A Penguin Special
How to Survive the Slump

CW00349985

Graham Bannock was born in London in 1932 but grew
up in Somerset and Dorset. He graduated in Economics
at LSE in 1955 after two years' military service and has
worked as a business economist, product planner and
market researcher, first at Ford, in Britain, then at the
Economist Intelligence Unit, Richard Thomas and
Baldwin, and the Rover Company. He left Rover for two
years at the OECD, but returned in 1962 as Head of
Economics and Market Research. After the Leyland-
Rover merger he went to Ford as Manager of the Market
Research Department and later as Manager of Advanced
Programs in the Product Development Group of Ford of
Europe Inc. From early in 1970 until September 1971 he
was Director of Research for the (Bolton) Committee of
Inquiry on Small Firms. He is now a partner in the
Economists Advisory Group. He has travelled widely and
has published (with A. J. Merrett) *Business Economics and
Statistics* (1962). He has also compiled *A Dictionary of
Economics* (with R. Rees and R. E. Baxter – Penguin,
1972) and has written *The Juggernauts: The Age of the
Big Corporation* (Pelican, 1973), as well as contributing
a number of articles to books and journals.

Graham Bannock

How to Survive
the Slump:
A Guide to Economic Crisis

Penguin Books

Penguin Books Ltd,
Harmondsworth, Middlesex, England
Penguin Books Inc., 7110 Ambassador Road,
Baltimore, Maryland 21207, U.S.A.
Penguin Books Australia Ltd,
Ringwood, Victoria, Australia
Penguin Books Canada Ltd, 41 Steelcase Road West,
Markham, Ontario, Canada
Penguin Books (N.Z.) Ltd,
182–190 Wairau Road, Auckland 10, New Zealand

Published in Penguin Books 1975

Made and printed in Great Britain by
Cox & Wyman Ltd, London, Reading and Fakenham
Set in Monotype Plantin

Contents

List of Charts

(N.B. Numbers in square brackets on charts refer
to column numbers in Appendix II.)

Acknowledgements

Because I wanted the text to be as brief and as uncluttered as possible I have given little acknowledgement to the work of others in a book that covers a very large field in the social sciences and finance. Some indication of my sources is given under the statistical tables and in the Notes on Further Reading at the end of the book.

Ron Baxter, Martin O'Donoghue, Jill Norman and Joe Roeber read and commented with remarkable speed upon an early draft of the manuscript. Victor Morgan also gave me some valuable advice on public finance and I have incurred a debt of unknown scale from many conversations with Sig Prais. Colette Cregan, Ian Hafekost, Diane Crosbie and Jacky Phasey all helped in various ways. I alone, of course, remain responsible for any remaining errors or omissions.

The Building Societies Association, the Department of National Savings, Johnson Matthey Limited, the Inland Revenue, Sharps Pixley Limited, The Standard Life Assurance Company, Samuel Montagu & Company and Sotheby & Company all gave me helpful advice or information.

The following organizations kindly gave permission to reproduce statistical material which is acknowledged at the appropriate place in the text: Consolidated Goldfields, H M S O, London and Cambridge Economic Service, Nationwide Building Society.

Introduction

Although, naturally enough, events have moved on since this book was completed (February 1975) I have not altered the text to take account of them before going to press (July 1975). In the intervening period the rate of inflation, taxes, share prices and unemployment went up and output and the foreign exchange value of the pound went down. The referendum on the E.E.C. gave a clear majority for staying in. As this book goes off to the printer, the Government is trying to secure agreement on an incomes policy. These events were to be expected; they do not affect the analysis I have made and indeed the reader would rightly suspect a book, designed to give long-term perspective to our problems, that required extensive rewriting after only five months.

It is no part of the purpose of this book to pontificate about what society should do but perhaps I should state my prejudices (which will already be familiar to readers of *The Juggernauts*) and which can be summed up as a hearty scepticism about the advantages of, and the necessity for, centralization. I believe that the solution to our problems is most likely to be found in a decentralization of our economic, social and political institutions.

It is often said that the acuteness of the contemporary economic problem in Britain is attributable to some inherent and unique deficiency in British society. This is very unlikely: Britain was the first country in modern times to achieve individual freedom and so break out of the medieval mould and into the industrial revolution. If the view of economic and social development put forward in this book is anywhere near the truth, Britain is simply the country where the processes described have been at work the longest. This, at least, gives us the chance to solve the problem first.

The first purpose of this book, I wish to emphasize, is to

provide *long-term* perspective to the economic problems of today and the political debate that surrounds them. The second purpose is to give an outline of the way in which long-term trends and the shorter-term economic prospect impinge upon the individual, his choice of job, his way of life and where he puts his savings. I started off with the second purpose alone, but soon realized that in a changing and confusing world, any attempt to give advice on, say, personal investment, without making clear the view of economic development upon which it is based, is like sending a man off into the wilderness with instructions but without a map: if he misses one landmark, or something unforeseen turns up, he is lost. The two purposes are, however, tackled separately in the two main parts of the book. Survival comes first, in Part I, and this part, dealing as it does with eminently practical matters, should be fairly straightforward for the general reader. But I hope that this will stimulate him to read on for a bird's eye view of what is happening in Britain and the other developed market economies.

All this is a tall order in a short book directed at the general reader but, at the risk at some points of over-simplification, I have tried not to dodge some of the more technical aspects of economics where they have practical relevance. I make no apology for attempting to deal with monetary theory and home brewing in the same volume. Economics ought to be practical and more widely understood, for it is too important to be left to economists alone.

July 1975   Graham Bannock

Part I
Survival

1. Peering into the Near Future

Stag- and slump-flation

In the two and a half decades since the Second World War, Britain and the world economy have experienced a period of unprecedentedly sustained prosperity. There have, of course, been minor pauses or recessions from time to time. In Britain, which has been less prosperous than other advanced countries in this period, these recessions in economic growth have been associated with balance of payments crises, each of which seemed very serious at the time but which, like a hangover, were eventually shrugged off. It was and is possible to identify these crises and the quickening of the rate of increase in prices which preceded them as symptoms of a deeper disease which might one day erupt into a worse illness, from which recovery would be much more difficult.

This now seems to have happened. The health of the world economy, and Britain's, is now worse than at any time since the 1930s. At the time this is being written (March 1975) unemployment in the UK is over 800,000, and it is about eight million in the United States. Although industrial output in Britain in the latest available quarter is only 2·5 per cent down over the previous quarter, business confidence and investment are low and it is generally expected that economic conditions will continue to deteriorate. Things are not as bad as they were in the 1930s and it is unlikely that unemployment will be allowed to rise to the levels of the inter-war slump, but they are bad enough and they will get worse before they get better. To this extent, I should make clear, the slump in the title of this book has already arrived. Whether or not it ever reaches 1930s' proportions, there has already been a slump in business confidence that is probably as great as occurred then. The end of another era in economic affairs has begun.

The real slump, therefore, is the widespread collapse in confidence in the feasibility of achieving high employment, ever-increasing prosperity and stable prices, at least within the framework of the system of economic organization as it has evolved so far in the democratic market economies. Stable prices, of course, went a long time ago, but it was only in 1974 that inflation in peacetime Britain reached double figures and it is only in 1975 that the punishing implications of the continuing depreciation of currency at this rate are being brought home to a majority of the population. We are also (and this is happening in most other advanced countries) confronted for the first time with weakening output, investment and employment without any slackening in the rate of inflation. What has come to be called 'stag-flation' seems to be turning into 'slump-flation'. Perhaps the biggest crack in the edifice of our economic system is the break in confidence in the value of money. Currency has not collapsed, but it is beginning to be regarded with wider-eyed realism, and the illusion that money is an effective store of value is fading fast. Money-illusion is, however, too deeply entrenched to disappear quickly, and for this reason much of the first part of this book is devoted to coming to terms with inflation as it affects personal savings and investment.

Inflation is inevitable in the industrial societies of the market economies as they have developed; it cannot be cured by tinkering with margin controls, exchange rates, money supply or voluntary incomes policies and will, therefore, remain with us until more radical changes take place.

Spectacular but little-understood changes in economic organization have occurred already in the last hundred years. The private sector of the economy has progressively come under the control of a relatively small number of large companies, great trade unions have emerged to negotiate the pay and conditions of employees, and the state itself has grown to intervene more and more in all economic activity. The state, of course, is all-pervasive now, but under it the economy divides clearly, if not precisely, into two sectors. The planned or post-competitive sector, with which the state is inevitably most closely linked and most sympathetic, consists of large companies (including state corporations) managed largely by salaried directors and executives who, both because they are not owners of the businesses they run and because of the exposed position of such large companies in society, are concerned more with reconciling conflicting social interests and their own security than with pursuing profit. The majority of the employees of these giant companies are organized in trade unions.

The companies themselves do not compete with one another to serve the consumer in the traditional sense; they coexist in a balance of power and jointly supply consumer needs in, as far as possible, a planned and regulated way. Their employees do not compete with one another for employment but are organized in trade unions to supply labour on negotiated terms, and each trade union coexists with others in a balance of power. Alongside, or rather interspersed within, this planned sector of the economy is the older market or competitive sector which more closely resembles the individualistic, unregulated, profit-seeking model which most people have in mind when they think of the capitalist system. The men and women who run these (generally small and very numerous) companies also own them, and their employees are not unionized. The incomes and activities of both employers and employees are determined by competitive forces rather than the explicitly or implicitly negotiated balance of power which reigns in the post-competitive sector.

The steady absorption of the competitive by the planned sector over the past hundred years or so has been accompanied (though not caused) by an enormous increase in the prosperity of the average person, and it is this prosperity which, through releasing demands in the democratic system for more security and participation, has brought about the growth of the state. This growth in public intervention is in turn the most important cause of the changes I have been describing and an important part of the mechanism through which persistently rising prices have become inseparable from the present social and economic system. This complex mechanism is described in Part II, but what it amounts to is that in the planned sector, where inflation originates, companies, trade unions and the state are all demanding more real resources and exercising their bargaining power to obtain them; these demands create tensions which have been resolved by making more money available and thus prices of goods and services have risen in money terms.

This process is not confined to Britain: the changes in social and economic organization I have referred to are common to all the advanced 'market' economies and, indeed, the opening up of the world economy, which freer trade and improved transport and communications have brought about so rapidly in the last three decades, has ensured the rapid transmission of the disease throughout the Western world.

The short-term outlook

We have now arrived at a point in Britain where one of the sources of tension – unemployment – cannot be resolved by inflating the general level of demand, because prices are already regarded as rising unacceptably fast. In February 1975 the retail price index stood at 20 per cent above the level of a year earlier. Because of this the government has allowed the recession to deepen without taking further action to boost demand.[1]

The immediate outlook, therefore, is for output to decline slowly and for unemployment to rise. This situation is likely to continue perhaps until the spring of 1976. At the same time prices will continue to rise as wage and other cost increases that occurred in 1974 and those already planned or anticipated in 1975, such as increased postal, rail and gas charges, work their way through the system. I have written 'will' rise rather than 'are likely to rise' simply because it is almost inconceivable that there will be widespread cost and price reductions in the modern or post-competitive sector of the economy. Contemporary conditions are completely different in this respect from those of the nineteenth century. Money wage declines in the post-competitive sector will be totally resisted by the trade unions, and in fact continuing increases are confidently expected. Some other costs such as those of certain imported raw materials could fall, but many material costs will continue to rise and low-capacity utilization will also raise unit costs. In these circumstances manufacturers will be obliged to raise prices if they are to avoid trading at a loss. Attempts to increase sales by holding prices constant or reducing them, and thus to increase capacity utilization and reduce unit costs, are not likely to be made by large firms in concentrated markets. This is because

1. The reader who finds it difficult to understand the dilemma between increasing employment and restraining inflation will find it explained more fully in Chapters 6 and 8.

they know that such action would be matched by their competitors. Nothing would be gained by any individual firm and all would lose.

In these circumstances investment will remain low and the economy stagnate. Rising prices will be accompanied by an increase in unemployment as output declines, but increased wages for those in employment and increased social security payments will prevent total expenditure and output from declining catastrophically.

This is the outlook for the short term – the period that will extend to at least a few months after this book is published. What will happen thereafter will depend very much upon the policies that the government decides to adopt, and these in turn will be affected by the course of events outside Britain.

Britain's external position

As far as practicable I shall avoid introducing the complications of Britain's external position, and in Part II I shall discuss the mechanism of boom, slump and inflation mainly as if Britain were a closed economy. This is a justifiable simplification in describing how the mechanism works because taking account of foreign trade and capital movements in fact complicates but does not alter the basic picture. However, in assessing the immediate outlook it is not possible to abstract from the external position. Britain exports goods and services and receives payment in return for them. She also imports goods and services and has to pay for them. In addition she both lends and borrows abroad. These flows have to balance: if the total value of exports, plus borrowing from abroad, is greater than the total value of imports, plus lending abroad, then the difference has to be made up by drawing on reserves of gold or foreign exchange.

The prices at which Britain exports are determined by the net effect of changes in the domestic level of prices and movements in the exchange rates between the pound and foreign currencies. Import prices are determined by price-levels in other countries and the exchange rates. At the present time the exchange rate for sterling is not fixed but is floating; that is to say, it is determined by the supply and demand. If the value of British exports of goods and services falls short of that of imports, then the demand for pounds sterling abroad to pay for exports from Britain will be less than the supply of pounds being offered by Britain for its imports. This will depress the value of the pound in terms of foreign currencies. This in turn will mean that the cost of imports into Britain will rise because the pound will buy less overseas and the cost of British exports to other countries in terms of their own currencies will fall. Thus, these changes in the exchange rate will tend to help correct the imbalance of trade by discouraging imports and stimulating exports. The extent to which this will happen depends partly upon the relative sensitivity of the demand for imports and exports to price changes. But the higher cost of imports will also raise the costs of imported raw materials, foodstuffs and other goods and services. Unless other costs such as wages rise relatively slowly, increases in domestic and export prices may offset the fall in the exchange rate. To this extent, therefore, changes in the exchange rate may not help the competitiveness of exports if the domestic price level is rising more rapidly than in other countries.

This is important because it means that just as the stimulation of demand at home to create employment is limited by inflation, the use of the exchange rate to insulate export prices from domestic price changes is limited by the feedback of import prices on domestic costs. This is particularly limiting for Britain, for which foreign trade is such a large proportion of total activity and which is obliged to import a very large proportion of its food, fuels and raw materials.

The overseas trade and payments position is further complicated by capital flows in and out of the country, but again these flows do not, except in the short term, affect the underlying realities of inflation and the factors that determine the domestic level of activity. In 1973, for example, Britain had a deficit on overseas current account of £1·2 billion, but the currency flow into the country was over £1·4 billion, so that official reserves rose by over £200 million. In 1974, the first full year following the increase in world oil prices, the deficit and offsetting currency flows were larger still. What has been happening is that, although Britain has exported less than she has imported, overseas countries have placed large sums of money in Britain which have more than made up the difference. This money, much of which consists of the surplus funds of the oil-producing countries, is attracted to London by high interest rates and the services provided by the London capital market.

Whilst allowing the UK economy more time to adjust to the need for a larger shift in resources to exports, these capital inflows create two problems. First of all, they add to the interest burden payable by Britain on its overseas debt, and, secondly, they increase the vulnerability of the economy to a change in overseas confidence in the pound. What this means is that if for any reason confidence in the British economy fell (or, to be more accurate, fell further) much of this short-term money (which includes money held in sterling by speculators anticipating future movements of the exchange rate) would be withdrawn so that it could be placed in stronger currencies elsewhere. This would precipitate a crisis, since it would result in a net outflow of currency and the exchange value of the pound would plummet downwards. In order to regain control of the exchange rate (which would be necessary if the alternatives of hyper-inflation[1] or an even sharper recession were to be avoided) the government would be forced to take very severe action. This might include the introduction of an incomes freeze, rationing with subsidies, and possibly import controls.

No one is able to predict with any accuracy whether a crisis of this kind will occur. Provided the government's hand is not forced by a capital outflow in this way it seems likely that the deepening recession will continue to the point where the rate of price increases will begin to slow down quite markedly, although prices should continue to increase. At this point the government might take action to reflate demand again to arrest the increase in unemployment. It takes time for public action of this sort to work through, however, and reflation in 1975 would not take effect until some time in 1976 when prices might begin to rise faster again. This may well produce a crisis in 1977 or later, but the chain of events will be influenced by what happens to the level of

1. There is no generally accepted definition of the term hyper-inflation. Hyper- means 'in excess', or 'beyond measure', according to the Oxford English Dictionary.

world trade, which will affect Britain's ability to export, and to the world monetary system.

Since almost all the advanced countries are experiencing recession with continuing inflation and since the US, the UK, Italy, France, and perhaps temporarily Japan, all have adverse overall balances of payments on current account, the outlook for world trade is extremely unfavourable. World trade in 1974 actually declined in real terms – the first decline in the post-war period – and the Organization for Economic Cooperation and Development (OECD) did not expect, in March 1975, that there would be any real growth at all in output in its member countries, which include most of the advanced market economies of the Western world. All of these countries are suffering from inflationary pressures which will inhibit them from expanding demand, and hence imports, while all of them need to increase exports. In this situation, when the need to maintain employment will not allow countries to avoid some action to stimulate demand, there is plainly a risk that they will resort to import controls. This would lead to a 'beggar-my-neighbour' situation in which all countries would try to restrict imports and expand exports, and a further decline of this sort would have particularly severe repercussions on Britain, and also on other countries which are heavily dependent on foreign trade, such as Japan. So far there is no clear sign that this will happen. Import controls are being discussed in Britain but the United States and other countries are now reflating without any attempt to restrict imports by physical controls.

Government policy

It looks as if we can expect varying rates of inflation and fluctuations in output as governments oscillate between giving priority to measures to control inflation and to control unemployment. The timing and amplitude of these oscillations is impossible to predict. It is not likely, however, that this cycle will be repeated many times without major changes in policy, because inflation will tend to get out of control, which would lead to the virtual breakdown of the currency and the economic system.

It is fairly safe to predict that most changes in policy, in Britain particularly, will be in the direction of more state intervention in economic affairs. This intervention will appear necessary not only from the course of economic events but also because of increasing demands from the electorate for protection against the effects of inflation and unemployment. The most likely outcome is that controls over prices and profits will be maintained in some form and some control over prices and incomes will be introduced. Interest is already turning from attempts to control economic activity through action on overall demand and investment to direct attempts to influence investment, employment and prices in particular industries. The 1975 Industry Bill, which greatly increases the government's powers in industry, typifies this trend. We may also expect a number of measures to reduce the impact of inflation upon tax rates, savings, corporate profitability and contractual obligations.

What form these measures will take and how widespread they will be it is difficult to say, because it will partly depend upon the rate at which prices continue to rise. The government has already announced that it will introduce a scheme for inflation protection for small savings in 1975, and some relief has been given to the effects of inflation on corporate taxation of stock appreciation. The use of inflation protection clauses in private contracts is already growing. Wider protection of savings, however, will require government action to relate returns on its own borrowings to inflation. This will greatly increase the cost of government borrowing and we can be sure that it will be delayed as long as possible, just as any automatic adjustment of tax allowances and rates will also be delayed if practicable. It will not be possible for private borrowers to offer similar protection until the government has acted, so extensive inflation protection of savings (indexation) will take some time to put into effect. Introduction will probably be progressive, but it must come if money savings are to continue to be made on any scale.

Price and other controls coming on top of changes resulting from the absorption of the market sector by the planned sector have already had considerable effects upon the variety and quality of goods available. Increased direct intervention in the economy and continued control of prices, profits and incomes will inevitably reduce further the sensitivity of output to demand, so continual shortages of particular goods and services are to be expected. These shortages may well be compounded in some cases by import controls and labour disputes.

History will not repeat itself

The outlook described here is far from cheerful, although it is not as gloomy as many of the predictions that have been made recently. It will be noted that I am predicting that output and employment will fall and then stagnate, probably with some fluctuations and with continuation of inflation, also at a fluctuating rate. It is unlikely that either employment or output will fall as much as in the 1930s. This is because governments now have both the means and the will to intervene in domestic affairs and because international cooperation will probably be sufficient to prevent a collapse of the international monetary system. A great deal has been learned about international economic cooperation since the Second World War and although economic nationalism will undoubtedly result in action being taken late, the prospect is that the worst will be averted. The crisis will, however, be prolonged and painful and, as in the 1930s, some countries will suffer more than others. Britain will be one of the worst sufferers and, again as in the 1930s, the effects will be concentrated upon particular industries and particular groups in society.

It is true that there is a very real possibility of social strife, the emergence of authoritarian régimes and a considerable loss of individual freedom. Social strife is always possible when the interests of some groups in society suffer more than those of others, and particularly so at the end of a very long period of rising living-standards during which aspirations have also steadily risen. Indeed, some loss of individual freedom has already occurred and more is implicit in the extension of the influence of the state which is foreseen. Social strife and authoritarianism are not things the individual can do much about, and I devote little space to these possibilities. In any event, I prefer to take an optimistic view of the evolutionary potential of the Western social and economic system.

It seems, however, in the light of the very deep rooted trends to be described in Part II, that there will not be the rapid return to sound money, fuller use of the market mechanism and withdrawal of state intervention that is advocated by many distinguished economists. Such a policy could only be introduced gradually over a very long period. It would require the overthrow of deeply entrenched vested interests on both the right and the left and, particularly since the early effects might be even more painful than continuing on the present path, it would be difficult to obtain continuing support from the electorate.

I now turn to a survey of some of the practical implications for the individual and his employment, spending and saving, of the course of events predicted.

2. Income, Employment and Expenditure

The sea change

A basic change has now taken place in economic life and the individual has to ask himself how he will be affected and what he should do about it. Deeply ingrained attitudes to money and how it can be earned and how it should be saved and spent may need revision. This is important because some rules of thumb which have been taken for granted may no longer be safe guides to behaviour. For example, in the past twenty years of steadily rising prosperity and prices it has been a safe rule that borrowing to finance property purchase is greatly to the advantage of the borrower. Many people have now discovered that this depends upon both income and property prices continuing to rise faster than the cost of borrowing.

Most serious is the situation where incomes and house prices cease to rise or actually fall, and interest rates rise. In these circumstances a borrower may find himself faced with the necessity of selling his house at a loss because he cannot afford the mortgage payments. If his income keeps up, however, he may be able to afford the increased payments and hope that the appreciation of his asset will one day be resumed. In the prolonged inflation that is expected, most, if not all, physical assets should appreciate, but borrowing is only wise if income is reasonably secure and keeping pace with the general price level.

Maintaining income is therefore vital. This may appear to be a statement of the obvious, but in a period of stag-flation, when it may be difficult to realize capital assets and when income from capital will be depressed, either by the erosion of fixed interest payments by inflation or by the pressure on dividends of increased costs, government controls and taxation, the maintenance of 'earned' income will be vital, even for those fortunate enough to have some capital.

The self-employed

The self-employed person is particularly vulnerable to stagflation. The state is prepared to assist large firms in financial difficulty but it will not intervene to support small firms in similar circumstances. If business is very bad the self-employed person will not be able to draw unemployment benefit unless he ceases to be self-employed; nor, as I shall explain later, is he as well placed as an employed person to secure an inflation-proof pension. The self-employed do, of course, enjoy important advantages. They have a freedom and, typically, a job satisfaction which is denied the average employee in a large concern. It is also, in a period of inflation, an advantage to pay taxes some fifteen months in arrears. However, for the majority of self-employed this tax advantage is offset by the recent introduction of an earnings-related contribution which is not linked to any social security benefits and is, therefore, a supplementary tax. The price of freedom for the self-employed is that they have to bear the burden of taxation and many of the regulations and administrative impositions of the state without enjoying many of the benefits which the state confers on employees and employers in large companies. Moreover, the self-employed for the most part depend for their income upon payments by customers and are directly vulnerable to bad debts and delays in the settlement of sums owed to them: a not unimportant consideration in a period of economic recession.

The self-employed and those who work in smaller companies are not weak because they are economically unimportant but because they have little bargaining power. As a group, the self-employed account for only 8 per cent of the labour force (approaching 2 million people), although private (as distinct from public) companies and businesses in all account for nearly half of all employment in the private sector. The markets in which the vast majority of these small firms compete are fragmented. The businesses concerned have to take the going price for their goods and services and can exert little or no influence over their market. They will meet resistance in passing on increased costs to their customers, especially under conditions of stagnating demand when their competitors will all be doing their best to increase

27

their own shares of the market. Some of their suppliers will by contrast be large firms with which they will have little or no bargaining power and whose increased costs will be passed on to them. Small retail shops, for example, cannot buy their stock from their suppliers on such advantageous terms as chain supermarkets because their purchasing power is individually so small. At the same time their ability to pass on higher prices will be limited by competition both from the supermarkets with lower costs and from other small shops. In a recession customers are likely to be more price-conscious than ever, so that the squeeze on small retailers which has been going on now for many years can be expected to intensify.

At the same time as being weak in the market place, small firms and their proprietors are politically weak, since they are not as well organized as the employers and employees of large companies. Because of this they have not had a voice in economic policy-making commensurate with their role in the economy, and their interests have suffered accordingly.

There is, in fact, ample evidence that the number of small firms and their share of employment has been declining, and there is some evidence that there has been a transfer of incomes away from both the proprietors of small firms and their employees to large firms and their employees. The typical self-employed person is not, of course, a well-to-do company director of a successful factory but a shopkeeper, plumber or market gardener whose total income may be considerably less than average adult earnings in the manufacturing and mining industries.

Because small firms tend to be more labour-intensive than large firms, are less able to borrow money at fixed interest, meet with more resistance in passing on increased costs and are less able to offer resistance to increased charges from suppliers, their proprietors are more likely to suffer from inflation and, for this reason, to be less ambivalent than most other sectors of society in their hostility towards it. Although the self-employed have, like everyone else, been cushioned to some extent from the effects of inflation by increased demands for their services while economic growth continued, the recession with continued inflation is intensifying the squeeze on the small firm sector by reducing that demand. The effects of the recession on small firms may therefore be more severe than in the inter-war period when prices were falling.

Little research has been carried out upon the effects of the inter-war depression upon small firms. To the extent that unemployment was heavily concentrated in iron and steel, coal, shipbuilding, textiles and other basic industries dominated by large firms, while employment in the service and distributive trades grew throughout the period, it appears that small firms suffered less than large.

Circumstances are very different now from what they were in the 1920s and 1930s. The number of small firms, in the distributive trades in particular, is falling rather than increasing. Financing them is more difficult now than it was then because taxation is higher. The number of sources of supply for small firms has also declined sharply following the merger-boom in the 1960s, and there are other adverse factors at work.

Even if small firms as a group find it difficult to cope with stagflation, some will prosper. Small firms are adaptable and can respond more quickly than large ones to the new opportunities which a sea change in the economic outlook always throws up. The individual must look out for these opportunities and many will find them. The most urgent thing for the self-employed to do, however, is to organize themselves into an effective bargaining group to try to improve their terms of trade with the rest of society. Although there are a large number of specialized associations for small businesses from farmers to veterinary surgeons, and some general ones such as the Smaller Businesses Association, each one represents only a tiny fraction of the total number of self-employed, even though some of them have a powerful voice in particular industries and professions. The self-employed, being by definition independent people, are reluctant joiners, but it is likely that continued economic pressure upon them will gradually overcome this reluctance. As others in society, having achieved an unprecedented degree of security, are demanding more freedom and more participation, so the self-employed will demand more security without wishing to relinquish their freedom.

The old and the retired

Another group of people which is even more vulnerable to inflation is, of course, the retired, living on the state pension supplemented in some cases by fixed incomes from invested savings or from employment pensions. State pensions are paid to almost 7·75 million people in Britain, and a significant number of others below retirement age draw private pensions or live off their savings. Some of the more active among the retired can supplement their pensions by taking employment, and their pensions are not affected if these earnings do not exceed £13 per week. In a stagnant economy the elderly may, of course, find it more difficult to find work. Their plight has now been recognized in Britain, and it looks as if the basic state pension, though hopelessly inadequate for anyone without free accommodation, their own house or another source of income, will not be allowed to be eroded by inflation.

For most people now working the basic state pension is only part of the income they can expect when they retire. Most will be members of an occupational pension scheme or will participate in an earnings-related state pension scheme. There has been a great deal of confusion over the state supplementary scheme and, at the time of writing, it seems certain that it will be confirmed as a contributory scheme in which the pensions of one generation will be financed by the contributions, from employers and employees of later generations, rather than out of the income of an invested fund. In this way contributions, and hence current pensions, can easily be increased as prices rise.

Civil servants already have pensions fully indexed to the cost of living, but it will not be possible for private occupational schemes, which are based upon invested funds, to provide inflation-proof pensions if inflation continues at recent levels. This is because fund managers will not be able to find investments from which income will rise fast enough (see Chapters 3 and 5) to keep pace with prices. In 1974-5 many companies transferred large sums from profit and loss accounts to pension funds to make up for deficiencies in the incomes of these funds, and they will be obliged to continue to do this if prices continue to rise at recent rates. Many firms, however, may not be able to do this and if inflation continues, as I expect, it will no longer be in the interest of companies or their employees to opt for private rather than state schemes. For the individual, at least, the old belief that nothing offered by the state is ever a bargain may be discredited under conditions of rapid inflation.

What is true for employees will also be true for the self-employed. In the past the self-employed have taken advantage of tax reliefs to contribute to private pension schemes, such as those offered by insurance companies, or have preferred to invest the money in their own businesses. In the future, they too may be well-advised to subscribe to the state supplementary scheme for at least part of their pension. Although not eligible for this as proprietors or partnerships, the self-employed can become eligible by incorporating their businesses, if they have not already done so, and paying themselves director's salaries from which deductions for the state pension scheme may be made. It will, of course, be necessary to file accounts at Company's House which will result in some loss of privacy: this is the price of limited liability, and there are other considerations.[1]

The unfortunate who are too old to benefit fully from state supplementary schemes and who are not members of an occupational pension scheme, or who wish to supplement the two state schemes, will have to do the best they can by investing in insurance-based pension schemes or the other forms of investment discussed in the next three chapters. Those who decide on private pension schemes should select ones that have a 'with-profit' element that will provide at least some protection against inflation, and they should bear in mind that it is a condition of the tax relief on such schemes that the capital cannot be withdrawn.

1. The self-employed person will need to look into this carefully for, as usual in these matters, the rules have not been framed to make the choice clear. It costs £20 a year to register a company and he will, if he incorporates, be liable for an employee's as well as his own contribution. His company will get tax relief on the employer's contribution, however, and he will get an inflation-proof pension, whereas if he retains self-employed status he will pay a graduated contribution which brings him no pension benefit.

Those who are concurrently trading on their own account and employed by someone else will have to be particularly careful because they will be liable to pay both self-employed and employee's contributions up to a specified maximum.

This means that they could find themselves locked into schemes which, under increasing inflation rates, might offer a declining income in real terms. They should certainly avoid the purchase of annuities, which are simply a form of fixed interest security from which the capital is not normally recoverable. However, see the section on indexation (pages 63–5) for a more profitable alternative.

The employee and industrial change

For the employee, stag-flation will provide a continuing threat to his job, but if he keeps his job and works for a large company he will be among the more favoured groups in society. In Britain unemployment will almost certainly not be allowed to rise to the levels of the 1930s, but it may be very high in some basic industries and particularly so in those industries which have benefited most from inflation, such as property and construction, or those where structural adjustments in response to changes in tastes or technology have been delayed by inflation. One of these is the motor industry, which is now in relative, if not absolute, decline. Some consumer and capital-goods industries heavily dependent upon the export trade could suffer badly if this contracts severely.

Again, the pattern will be very different from the 1930s. Building and construction, the motor industry and others such as chemicals and rayon, together with the service and distributive trades, were growing fairly fast, at least after 1932; these industries are less well-placed in the 1970s. On the other hand, some which suffered badly in the 1930s – especially coal-mining – could be little affected in the 1970s. Others, for example the steel industry, could be hit really hard for a second time. Others again, such as those concerned with supplying North Sea oil, energy conservation and nuclear power industries, will presumably continue to grow. In the 1970s, as in the 1930s, food, drink, tobacco and clothing – the basic consumer industries – will probably hold up fairly well. Finally, the trend to state intervention is likely to lead to a continuing growth in public employment, and anyone who really wants his job to be as safe as possible ought to enter the Civil Service.

Industries tend to be concentrated geographically, so in a recession, where some industries are more affected than others, unemployment is also concentrated. This is because the direct employment effects of recession in particular industries are reinforced by the local multiplier effects of declining expenditure by those out of work. In 1932, the worst year of the depression, unemployment in Scotland as a percentage of the labour force was more than double that in the south-east of England, and in Wales it was nearly three times as high. This pattern will not necessarily be repeated. Scotland as a whole is now in a much stronger position economically than it was in the 1930s because of the growth of energy industries, while other parts of the country, for example the Midlands, in which the motor industry is so important, are less well-placed. But even within broad regions there will be large differences in the pattern of unemployment. For example, in the 1930s unemployment in Scotland was heavily concentrated in the heavy industries in the south-west and along the Clyde, while eastern Scotland and the Edinburgh region were relatively prosperous. In the present case the pattern may well be repeated, since it is in the east that the benefits of the boom in North Sea oil are being felt the most.

The individual threatened by unemployment should, for this reason, be prepared to consider moving to another area where jobs are available. Between 1923 and 1936 1·1 million people moved into London, the south-east and the Home Counties from the rest of the country and stayed there. Moving home is not an easy decision. Some people can hardly bear to pull up their roots and there are always practical difficulties in the way, but it may help to consider whether or not local ties are being over-valued because work is unsatisfying or non-existent. New and more satisfying work can do much to compensate for, and eventually to outweigh, a domestic upheaval. The fatal weakness in our over-centralized society is that for so many – probably most – work is a drudge or a bore rather than an important and satisfying part of life.

All this is equally applicable to the white- as to the blue-collar worker. Although unemployment may have been low, the 1960s saw much reorganization coming about through mergers which were often accompanied by redundancies, not only among manual workers but also, and often to a greater extent, among management and clerical workers. Although there were many personal tragedies, many also found that they had been dead-alive in their old jobs, and the challenge of looking for new work actually released them to realize dreams that they had almost given up. The tragedies arose when it was the least resilient who lost their jobs, leaving some of those who would have benefited from a change amongst the unscathed.

Value for money

Even for those fortunate enough to be fully employed there is, as I have shown, the possibility of a decline in real disposable incomes followed by a period of unknown length in which real disposable incomes will almost certainly grow more slowly than they have in the last two decades. This means that everyone will have reason to be more careful about how money is spent. There have also been some important changes that affect spending and where and on what money is spent.

One of the consequences of the decline in competition which has accompanied the concentration of industry into the large units which characterize the modern economy has been the emergence of widening differentials between relative prices. This has been reinforced, paradoxically, by the abandonment of resale price maintenance. This does not only mean that the same goods or services may be available at widely differing prices in different places (although this remains true, with the recent advent of price control some differentials may have narrowed) but that the quality and choice of goods and services available varies widely.

Quality is difficult to measure, and economists have always dodged the difficulty by assuming, with good reason, that the consumer is the best judge and that his decisions will be reflected in the prices he is prepared to pay for things. It is further assumed that, although it is not possible to compare the amount of satisfaction between consumers (which depends upon the quality and variety of goods consumed as well as the quantity), each consumer will buy that combination of goods at market prices that maximizes his overall satisfaction. All this, however, assumes that consumers know what goods are available at what prices, and that free competition exists among producers and retailers to supply their needs.

In contemporary society, however, these assumptions no longer hold. Confronted with a 100-gramme packet of Supersol with magic ingredient X at 75p and a Sainsbury's own brand 125-gramme packet (without magic ingredient X) at 85p, he may well be uncertain as to which will give him most satisfaction. Even more complex assessments that he will not really be qualified to make will be required when he comes to buy a motor car or a colour television. A less complex decision, and perhaps a better illustration of the point I am trying to make, will face him when he goes into his local pub, orders a pint of draught bitter and is told that only keg is available because the brewer that owns the house has stopped supplying draught beer. Under conditions where consumer choice is highly influenced, if not determined, by the producer, the assessment of quality becomes very important. Competition never did fully safeguard the consumers' interests, but it is less effective today than it ever was, and the growing number of consumer-protection measures introduced by the State is a reflection of this.

What this boils down to is that the consumer will have to work even harder than he has in the past to get best value for his money. It also means, incidentally, that official statistics of the national product and of retail prices are much more difficult to interpret than might at first appear. A rise in the national income, for example, only means that people are better off if they are able to spend that increment on things that give them more satisfaction. Although (contrary to the views of those who suspect all information from governments) totally innocent in intent, official statistics are full of pitfalls for the unwary, who usually, interpreting them like those who prepare them, assume perfect competition and an economic and social environment which has long since gone.

The market place

Because of the coexistence and interdependence of the older and new types of economic organization, the workings of markets and their implications for consumer purchasing are somewhat involved; but it is worth making the effort to unravel them, for there are some real practical benefits to be gained.

There are, in effect, two distinct types of market; what Professor Hicks calls *fixprice* and *flexprice* markets. In fixprice markets producers cost their products and add a margin to cover overheads and profit. They vary these prices as infrequently as possible and absorb temporary changes in their costs. Frozen-food manufacturers do not change the price of fish fingers or orange juice if, in one week, there is a big fall in the price of fish at Grimsby or of oranges at New Covent Garden market. In fact, large companies try to protect themselves as far as possible from fluctuations in supply and prices by securing their own sources of supply. Thus, one frozen-food manufacturer owns a large fishing fleet, another fruit and vegetable farms. The fish and vegetable markets, like the stock market and those for gold or foreign exchange, are flexprice markets. Price is determined by supply and demand in the market place. If the catch is exceptionally heavy the price of fish will tend to be lower than when the catch is poor.

What this suggests is that, wherever the choice is available, we should buy in fixprice markets at times of shortage and flexprice markets at other times; but it is more complicated than that because flexprice markets are primarily wholesale or professional markets, and therefore prices at any particular time tend to be substantially lower than in retail markets. Even when buying of goods that pass through a flexprice market is done at retail level, it is generally much cheaper to buy in the competitive sector than in the modern sector. This is because competition, and probably also specialization, are likely to keep down the margin between the wholesale price and the retail price. Thus lemons will be 25 per cent cheaper or even more in a street market such as Chapel Street in London (where supplies are drawn straight from New Covent Garden and sold by perhaps half a dozen competing street traders with very low overheads) than in a supermarket where packaging costs and higher overheads do not allow price competition with the street traders. In the same way, if he is a good buyer your local butcher will offer very competitive prices for meat and often far superior quality.

Manufactured goods, on the other hand, which do not normally pass through a flexprice market, will, as everyone knows usually be cheaper at the chain supermarket than elsewhere. This is because the chain can buy more cheaply from the manufacturer than the independent retail outlet is able to. However, competition between chains in the modern sector may not always be sufficient to drive down prices very far, and in fact studies carried out suggest that average prices are only a few per cent lower in large retail outlets than in smaller ones, although some individual prices may differ by 25 per cent or more. The marketing strategy of 'loss-leaders' also provides good buying opportunities for the selective, and it almost goes without saying that chain retailers' 'own brands' are usually much better buys than the branded products of the larger manufacturers. Very often they are identical, except for the packaging, because they are made by the same firm. The price gap exists because the giant retailer can drive a hard bargain over prices and because retailers' own brands do not have to bear the full costs of marketing incurred on manufacturers' brands. The manufacturers cannot do much about it and will often supply on condition that their brand-name is not used. They hope, usually with reason, that their marketing techniques and power will prevent price-cutting which would erode their share much further. Thus price-cutting by Jet (Conoco) petrol stations has not led to a petrol price-war among the major oil companies who prefer, for the good reasons explained more fully in Chapter 7, non-price competition with other weapons.

There are reasons for not neglecting the small shop in the search for best buys amongst manufactured goods as well as the other goods that originate in flexprice markets and which I have already discussed. This is because the giant retail chains are forced, in order to buy the vast quantities they need, to obtain most of their supplies from the largest manufacturers. The smaller retailers are free to draw upon the diminishing number of small manufacturers. Their products may be cheaper in some cases because competition may prevent them from increasing their prices, especially in recession, or for all sorts of other, more haphazard reasons. The reader may find this difficult to believe (see Chapter 7, page 122, for the theory of it) but it has been demonstrated in the United States that price behaviour in fragmented competitive industries is quite different from that in concentrated industries. The necessary research does not seem to have been carried out in Britain, but if you are lucky you will find evidence in the shops.

Minimizing purchasing costs should, of course, be an important part of everyone's strategy for maintaining standards of living under stag-flation. The first thing to do is to buy in bulk wherever possible and if the storage space is available: not only the obvious things like food, but other consumable items such as electric plugs or light bulbs, toothbrushes or garden requisites. Under conditions of recession you will find small shopkeepers and wholesalers more interested in striking a bargain and there are discount houses in most areas.

Hoarding as an investment

Bulk buying not only reduces purchase costs but also gives one minor and one other major benefit. The minor benefit is that by making fewer shopping trips or having things delivered you can save on petrol or bus fares. The major benefit is that by buying in advance you defer price increases. The two major benefits together result in substantial savings, as a little arithmetic will show. Let us assume that prices of preserved and processed foods are rising at 15 per cent per annum and that buying in bulk achieves a reduction in price of 25 per cent; buying supplies a year in advance then saves about 40 per cent in cost. This is a staggering tax-free return when the low risk is considered: compare it with the return on a deposit with a building society. It will clearly pay to borrow money from the bank at 15 per cent to invest in preserves and tinned goods: even if prices rise by less than expected or do not rise at all, the bulk-buying economics will still greatly exceed the cost of the loan. Two assumptions have to hold, however: that you have suitable storage space, and that the existence of stocks will not encourage you to increase consumption. If these hold, hoarding is one of the best possible investments that can be made in inflationary periods.

Freezers

By the use of a freezer the same principle can be applied to fresh food, but the economics are more complicated, and not so attractive unless you are prepared to work fairly hard at it and face some risk of loss through power cuts or breakdown. Let us assume that a freezer costs two units of electricity a week to run and that it will hold 20 lb. of food per cubic foot. An eight-cubic-foot freezer would hold about 160 lb. of food and cost 22p per week to run (at 1·35 per unit of electricity). Frozen food should not be kept for more than three months on average as flavour tends to deteriorate (although it remains safe to eat). We will assume that the stock is turned over four times a year. This limits savings due to deferment of price rises and it may also limit the quantity discounts obtained. But fruit and vegetables can be bought or, better still, taken straight from the garden for freezing when they are in season, and meat can be bought when it is best and cheapest. Ready-frozen food can also be bought in bulk at quite substantial savings from frozen-food centres. Discounts on fresh food are larger than those on preserves and fluctuate more because they are sold mainly in flexprice markets; it might be reasonable to assume buying savings of a third and inflation savings of about 3 per cent – say, £50 on food put through the freezer in a year. Against this, electricity would cost about £11 and something would have to be allowed for depreciation and, if you wished, £2–3 for insurance. You would have to pay perhaps £100 for the freezer and lay out £40 or so in working capital to keep it filled up.

The annual return on capital on these assumptions would be about 18 per cent after depreciation and before allowing for travel savings – well above the cost of borrowing the money, and a better tax-free return than you could get from any financial asset, but not as good as that on hoarding, and involving a much heavier work-load.

DIY and taxes

One other peculiarity of contemporary society, perhaps less obvious than the one I have just been writing about, is that the combined effect of higher taxes, changing wage differentials and changing technology is steadily eroding the basis of division of labour and specialization on which our economic system and standards of living are commonly supposed to depend. In short, most people will find that they can meet some of their own needs themselves more economically than if they pay for them out of earned income.

To illustrate this, let us imagine a person who earns £2,750 a year, or about £1·40 per hour before deductions. Let us suppose that this person is considering working overtime or taking a second job to help make ends meet. He should also consider spending that additional working-time to become more self-sufficient. Let us see what happens if he starts by making his own beer.

Using a kit which he can buy for 45p (and this is not the cheapest way of doing it) he can easily make sixteen pints of beer in less than an hour's work. This beer would cost him, even after allowing for the cost of sugar not included in the kit, less than 3½p per pint, compared with a retail price of 20–25p per pint. By an hour's work he would save an expenditure of at least £2·64 (i.e. 20p minus 3½p multiplied by 16). If he is lucky enough he may be able to work overtime at time and a half, or £2·10 per hour, so he is better off to the extent of 54p per hour if he stays at home. But this is before deductions: if we ignore graduated contributions (from which he will receive a pension benefit) and just look at income tax, we find that his take-home pay is much less than £2·10 per hour. A married man with one child will pay a marginal tax rate of about 33 per cent on earnings at this level, which means that 69p will go to the Inland Revenue. This more than doubles the savings he makes to £1·23 per hour!

If we allow for the fact that the person in our example does not have to leave his family to make his beer at home, that he will gain considerable satisfaction from doing it and that as soon as a little skill is acquired he will be making stronger and better beer at home than he can buy in the off-licence, then the case for self-sufficiency over that for working overtime is overwhelming. The advantage would be less for those with higher earnings, but at very high levels where marginal rates of tax are also high the savings increase again. A professional person, say a finance adviser, paid an hourly fee might well find that he would be better off making his beer or wine at home than advising on the intricacies of the capital transfer tax!

It might be thought that home brewing, because of the important excise-tax element in the price of beer, is unrepresentative of the advantages of self-sufficiency. It is also a particularly simple example because little or no special capital equipment or knowledge is required. But if you have a garden or can get an allotment you will find that equally striking cash savings and even greater non-monetary and quality benefits flow from growing some or all of your own vegetables. Many other things can be more cheaply done for oneself than bought in, and many are more easily done at home than ever before because of new materials, processes and hand tools. Home decoration, making yoghourt, picture-framing and all kinds of repair and maintenance work are examples.

A few people claim to be unable to do anything with their hands, but very few indeed cannot learn to do something creative if they really want to. Some of the examples in this chapter have been based on comparisons between spending time on self-sufficiency work and overtime or 'moonlighting', as the Americans call working at second jobs. For someone who does not have the opportunity to moonlight or cannot find work at all, self-sufficiency provides a net gain to his standard of living that would otherwise be denied him altogether.

The erosion of disposable income

Except in comparing the situation of the self-employed and the employee, I have not discussed taxation in this chapter, apart from showing that it very much affects decisions about doing things yourself or paying others to do them. But taxation is an important fact of modern life and must be constantly born in mind in taking all decisions about getting and spending. The burden of taxation is likely to increase still further in the next few years. Government expenditure plans for the period to 1978–9 clearly imply that taxes will be increased, even though the assumptions made about economic growth are optimistic. These increases may take the form of higher direct taxation (income tax) or indirect taxes (such as VAT) or, most probably, both. Local authorities are also facing considerable financing problems. In the short run further increases in rates are probable, and in the longer run either central government will have to assume greater responsibility for local expenditure (much of which it determines by state legislation or policy directives), or local authorities will need new sources of income, such as local income or sales taxes; unless, that is, expenditure is cut back.

Not much can be done to avoid rates – although there are anomalies in the rating system which can be exploited by the more mobile. Direct taxation is a different matter. Unless your affairs are unusually simple or you are exceptionally well-informed, then the chances are that you are paying more tax than the law requires and you should take professional advice.

The ratepayer and taxpayer can console himself with the thought that expropriation of income and wealth by both local authorities and central government has a very long history in this country, as in most others. The medieval king or baron whose staff or soldiers seized a few chickens or a coin or two from the peasant to finance a war had somewhat less respectable motives than his descendants today, although there will be many who feel that the purpose of present expropriation is not much more closely related to their own interests than that of earlier times. Since such an important proportion of your income is spent by public authorities of one kind or another it does, of course, make sense to use your vote where you can to influence that proportion and the way it is spent.

3. Savings and Investment: I

The principles of investment

Almost everyone needs to save. Motives for saving vary: it may be simply for emergencies; it may be for old age; or it may be to achieve some aim such as a holiday abroad. Whenever money is accumulated a decision has to be taken about the form in which it is to be kept; 80 per cent of the population aged over sixteen have savings held in some kind of financial asset, whether it be a current account at the bank or stocks and shares. Many will also have some physical or real assets such as houses or gold watches, but I defer consideration of these until the next chapter. After a brief review of the principles of investment, which are equally applicable in all cases, this chapter deals with the past record of investment in paper assets, and attempts in very general terms to show how the economic outlook should affect your choice of financial assets in the future.

In choosing investments it is essential to consider three factors in relation to your objectives: risk, real after-tax yield and liquidity. Usually risk is related to the return or yield on your investment: the higher the expected return the greater the risk, and vice versa. At least, this is the traditional view, based upon the assumption that profit is, in part, the reward for risk-taking. Thus the risk of total loss on a government (gilt-edged) security is negligible, while that on the unsecured debentures (fixed-interest securities) of a public company is perceptibly greater, and the yield will reflect this. On the stock exchange the prices of company debentures and gilt-edged securities reflect the fact that companies may go bankrupt and default, while the government will not do so. Since fixed-interest securities by definition pay an annual interest as a stated percentage of the par (or issued value) of the stock, the lower the price of the stock, the higher is the yield as measured by the fixed annual interest payment expressed as a percentage of the price of the stock. Thus the gross of tax-flat yield, as it is called, on 2·5 per cent consols was 15·36 per cent on 6 February 1975, and their price in the market £16·50.

Although there is little or no risk that the government will cease to pay interest on its debt or that it will fail to redeem it, there is clearly a risk of a loss in capital value if interest rates rise. Thus the price of consols, which are undated securities (that is to say the government does not undertake to redeem them), has fallen as interest rates have risen. 2·5 per cent consols could be bought for £73·50 in 1949 when they were yielding 3·30 per cent, £51·10 in 1959 when they yielded 4·95 per cent, and £23·20 in 1973 when the yield had risen to 10·85 per cent. Redeemable securities (where the borrower undertakes to repay the face value at a given date) provide, where the securities are bought at below that value, a bonus in terms of this capital payment. The calculation of the full yield – the running yield, as it is called for securities which are held to redemption – has to take this eventual repayment of capital into account.

Equity or ordinary shares do not have a fixed yield and carry the risk that the borrower will pay lower dividends next year than this or that he will not pay dividends at all. Companies may go into liquidation, possibly with no asset value remaining for the equity shareholders after other claims have been met. Yields on equities are normally lower than those on fixed-interest securities, however, because although risks of total loss are greater there is also a possibility that dividends, and hence the market price of the share, will increase in time and thus offer some hedge against inflation. On 6 February 1975 the average dividend yield on equities (the before-tax dividend as a percentage of the market price of the share) was 8·04 per cent. The yield on consols, as I have mentioned, was 15·36 per cent, a gap of 7·32 percentage points. This is called the *reverse yield gap* because prior to 1959 the yield on gilts was lower than that on equities, not the other way round as it is now.

The reversal of the yield gap between gilt-edged and equities reflects the market view that the low risks of gilt-edged in money terms are not sufficient to justify a lower yield than that of equities, which offer the prospect of a higher real return after the effects of inflation are taken into account. It is not enough to consider the money return on investments unless the investor anticipates that the purchasing power of money will remain constant.

In assessing yield, the investor has not only to consider nominal and real returns, but also after-tax returns. This further complicates the assessment. Most forms of investment, in effect, have income tax deducted from dividends or interest at source at the basic rate, but some do not; and some investments are liable to capital gains tax if they appreciate in value and some are not. It is not sufficient for the investor simply to calculate tax at the standard rate unless his marginal tax rate (the rate he pays on additional income) is equal to the standard rate, or, as it is at the time of writing, the basic rate of 33 per cent. Because of the complexities of allowances and frequently changing tax legislation most people have little idea what marginal rate of tax they are paying. It is, however, fairly easily established from tax tables or by asking the Inland Revenue, and this is an essential first step towards rational investment. Even fewer people understand capital gains taxation which is not, for an individual, necessarily a fixed rate of 30 per cent as is commonly supposed, even where he is liable for the tax. This rate is the maximum, because the taxpayer has the option of having half of the net gains taxed at his marginal rate of income tax. The analysis in this chapter assumes that the reader pays income tax at the standard rate. Some of the conclusions will differ for others.

Finally, the investor must consider liquidity, which may be broadly defined as the ease, speed and cost at which an asset can be turned into cash. Current accounts at banks are highly liquid because they can be withdrawn without notice and there are little or no transaction costs. Fixed-interest securities and equities can be sold on the stock exchange at any time, subject to stamp duty and stockbroker's commission, amounting to about 5 per cent in all on a small transaction. Real assets are less easily turned into cash and transaction costs are usually much higher.

The considerations of yield, risk and liquidity apply to any individual investment, but it will be obvious that a portfolio of several different kinds of investment can reduce risk and also provide different degrees of liquidity and yield. Risk can be reduced by spreading investments both among different investment media and among alternative investments for any given medium. For example, if you have only a little money to invest in equities it may

45

be wise to invest in a unit trust which spreads its funds over many shares, but it will also be wise not to put all your savings into equities in case this whole class of investment proves to be relatively unprofitable. In particular, your investment portfolio should achieve a balance of degrees of liquidity which accords with your likely needs. The market price of assets fluctuates and will continue to fluctuate. If you need cash quickly, you do not want to be forced to sell assets at a time when prices are temporarily depressed. Some money at least has to be held on deposit where it can be withdrawn quickly and without penalty. In this way the inclusion in your portfolio of relatively low-yielding assets which you can realize easily and cheaply can actually help you to achieve a higher overall average return than would otherwise be the case. In spreading investments you must, of course, bear in mind that the time you will have to spend on administration will, along with transaction costs, be greater the further your investment funds are spread.

This rapid survey of the principles of investment has not attempted to cover the practical details. These are not as difficult as they are often made out to be. The investor should take advice from his bank manager or accountant, or some other qualified person, on how exactly he should go about investing. If you are wise, you will also not commit large sums of money without talking over your choice of investment media with experts.

Whatever your source of advice, however, you should reserve some scope for the exercise of your own judgement over *what* you invest in, especially if you have firm convictions about your own needs or about the course of future events. Your own needs are vital. Whilst an expert may, for example, advise you that you will achieve a higher yield on equities than on building-society deposits, even if he is right you may well find that the higher yield is insufficient compensation for the mental anguish you suffer at watching your shares go up and down, and the worry and complication of dealing with the paperwork which inevitably accompanies direct investment in equities. Furthermore, although professional investment management involves extensive knowledge and often the use of systematic method, the record of professional investment management is not in general impressive. Except where that management can demonstrate an exceptional record on past performance (which may not of course be repeated in the future), the claims of professional investment managers should be treated with some scepticism. This is partly because the outcome of investment is dominated by political and economic events which no one can forecast with accuracy, and partly because, like other people, some investment advisers are better at their jobs than others. (Professional investment managers also face the difficulty that their purchases and sales of securities are often so large that they can move the market against themselves; when a major institution sells a large line of stock the price will be likely to fall.)

Deposits

There are many kinds of deposit facilities available through the clearing banks, the trustee savings banks (TSBs), the building societies, the finance houses, the Post Office and other institutions. They offer varying interest rates and tax treatment. Interest rates offered are subject to variation at short notice, but some of these institutions offer higher fixed rates for term deposits – that is, where notice is required before withdrawal. It is worth remembering that local-authority bonds and other short-dated fixed-interest securities, if held to maturity, offer precisely the same type of investment as a term deposit, and sometimes at more attractive interest rates. These facilities all offer guaranteed liquidity and protection from loss of the money value of capital. This protection is complete for public-sector institutions, and it is inconceivable that the government would allow a major clearing bank or a building society to fail. It is not unknown for other private-sector deposit-taking institutions to collapse, however.

In Table 1 I have assembled some examples of long-term rates of return on different assets. It can be seen that before the Second World War the combination of falling retail prices and prevailing interest rates meant that money placed either in a building society or the Post Office (now National Savings Bank) grew in real as well as money terms. The former gave a real return of 7·2 per cent between 1925 and 1939, and the latter 3·3 per cent. The return on building-society shares is free from tax for most taxpayers, as is

Index numbers 1925 = 100

| YEAR | PAPER ASSETS | | | | | | REAL ASSETS | | | | | | RETAIL PRICES |
| | National savings | | Building-society shares | | Industrial shares | | Older houses | | Gold | | English furniture | | |
	Money terms	Real terms	Money terms	Real terms	Money terms	Real terms	Money terms	Real terms	Money terms	Real terms	Money terms	Real terms	
1925	100	100	100	100	100	100	100	100	100	100	100	100	100
1939	145	158	244	265	204	222	100	109	181	197	57	62	92
1955	215	100	357	165	719	333	323	150	294	136	206	95	216
1965	275	94	503	172	2,051	702	571	196	295	101	524	179	292
1974	319	59	789	145	2,719	501	1,497	276	1,607	296	1,850	341	543

Table 1a: Money and Real Values of £100 Invested in Various Assets in the United Kingdom, 1925–74

Per cent increase (decrease)

	Total increase	Annual increase	Total increase	Annual increase	Total increase	Annual increase	Total increase	Annual increase	Total increase	Annual increase	Total increase	Annual increase	Total increase	Annual increase
1925–39	58	3·3	165	7·2	122	5·9	9	0·6	97	5·0	(38)	(2·3)	(8)	(0·6)
1939–55	(36)	(2·0)	(38)	(2·0)	51	2·6	38	2·0	(31)	(1·7)	54	2·7	135	5·5
1955–65	(6)	(0·6)	4	0·4	111	7·8	31	2·7	(26)	(2·3)	88	6·5	35	3·0
1965–74	(37)	(3·6)	(16)	(1·7)	(29)	(2·9)	41	3·9	193	12·7	91	7·5	86	7·1
1925–65	6	(0·1)	72	1·4	603	5·0	96	1·7	1	0·0	79	1·5	192	2·7
1955–74	(41)	(1·8)	(12)	(0·6)	50	2·2	84	3·3	118	4·2	259	7·0	151	5·0
1925–74	(41)	(0·7)	45	0·7	401	3·3	176	2·0	196	2·2	241	2·5	443	3·5

(For National Savings and Building Society accounts it is assumed that interest is not withdrawn but allowed to compound. For industrial shares it is assumed that after-tax dividends are re-invested.)
SOURCE: see Appendix I.

Table 1b: Total and Average Annual Rates of Change in The Real Value of Various Assets in the United Kingdom, 1925–74

that on National Savings.[1] Since the war, however, interest rates have failed to keep pace with the rate of inflation. This has more than wiped out the pre-war gains for anyone who had money in National Savings after the war. £100 deposited in 1925 would have *depreciated* in real terms at 0·7 per cent per annum over the whole period, and at 1·8 per cent per annum since 1955. The rate of interest for National Savings ordinary accounts remained at 2·5 per cent between 1925 and the end of 1970, being increased to 3·5 per cent in January 1971 and to 4 per cent in January 1973. Investment accounts were introduced towards the end of the period, offering higher interest for long-term savers, but these have not offered a real return either and the depositor has paid very dearly for the widespread withdrawal facilities offered by the Post Office.

Building societies have offered a real return of 0·7 per cent over the whole period 1925–74, but have failed to achieve a real return in the post-war period. Appendix II, which gives annual interest and inflation rates over the whole period, shows that building societies have offered a real rate of return in only ten of the past twenty-six years (1949–74), and not once in the last seven years.

Fixed-interest securities

Fixed-interest securities have also not given the investor a real return after tax in the post-war period. I have not included a representative fixed-interest security in Table 1 because Table 2 contains an unusually detailed, though now somewhat out-of-date, analysis of returns on consols made by two economists.

These figures show that the regular investor in consols would have received the substantial real return of 8·7 per cent before the Second World War. After the war the return disappeared altogether and was in fact negative, that is, −3·8 per cent, between 1939 and 1963. This would have been more than sufficient to wipe out any pre-war gains for the investor who stayed loyal to consols

1. Those liable for the investment-income surcharge of 15 per cent on investment incomes of over £2,000 a year or who pay income tax at a higher than standard rate may be liable for tax on building society interest. National Savings Bank interest of up to £40 a year is free of tax.

throughout the period. (The method of calculation is somewhat different from that used by me in Table 1, since mine are based upon the investment of a lump sum, and the periods taken are also different. These differences do not, however, affect the general

	Equities				Consols			
	Money terms	Real terms			Money terms	Real terms		
			High	Low			High	Low
Average 1919–38	8·7	10·9	14·7	7·9	6·6	8·7	10·8	5·2
Average 1945–63	11·6	7·6	13·2	1·5	(1·9)	(5·3)	(1·9)	(−7·8)
Total 1919–63	8·0	5·8			1·4	(1·4)		
Total 1939–63	9·1	5·0			(0·4)	(3·8)		

Per cent p.a. compound increase (decrease)

Table 2: Achieved Net-of-Tax Real and Money Rates of Return on Equities and Consols, 1919–63

(The authors assumed for the purposes of these calculations that an equal sum in real terms was invested at the beginning of each year in a representative share index and 2·5 per cent consols. At the end of the period the securities are presumed to be sold and the rates of return are those rates of interest at which the sums of money would have to be invested to realize the net of tax dividends plus the net of tax capital gains or losses incurred. The averages given above are averages of successive ten-year periods in which this exercise was carried out, while the total figures relate to the exercise carried out over the whole period stated.)

SOURCE: A. J. Merrett and Allen Sykes, 'Return on Equities and Fixed Interest Securities, 1919–1963', *District Bank Review*, December 1963

conclusions drawn.) A somewhat better performance could have been achieved by investment in short-dated securities, and an even better performance if opportunities had been taken to sell securities when prices were high and repurchase them when they were low. However, the investor would have had to be very active and lucky to have achieved a real return on government securities in the post-war period as a whole.

Equities

As long-term investments, fixed-interest securities have been a disaster in the post-war period, and gains before the war have been insufficient to offset losses afterwards. It has proved possible to maintain the real value of capital through building-society deposits over the whole period, but not since the war. Equity investments have, however, performed much better than any of the interest-bearing media, both before and, more particularly, after the war. Table 2 in fact shows that the real return on equities before the war was four times that on consols, while after the war equities would have made money at a much faster rate than fixed-interest investments would have lost it. Equity market values do, of course, fluctuate more than those of fixed-interest securities. The table shows that the spread between high and low decennial returns for equities was much greater than that for consols after the Second World War, but the return was always positive for equities and always negative for consols.

Table 1 includes my own, less refined, calculations of the return on ordinary shares from 1925 to 1974. These are based upon the value of a lump sum invested in a representative share index, plus accruing dividends reinvested and minus income tax at a constant standard rate. These also show positive returns over the whole period and as a whole after the war.

In the past, despite fluctuations in share prices, those who have held on grimly to their equities have done relatively well in the long run. Chart 1 shows how great these fluctuations in share prices have been over the last fifty years and how much of the increase in the index has simply reflected inflation. Nevertheless, the underlying trend in real share prices has been gently upwards. Even in 1974 after the 1973–4 stock market crash – the biggest ever in Britain – the £100 invested in 1925 would still have been worth £90 in real terms, even without taking accrued dividends into account. A similar investment in fixed-interest securities (2½ per cent consols) would be worth £40 in real terms. As I have already shown, when dividends are taken into account, equities, unlike fixed-interest securities, show a significant real return in the postwar period. As can be seen from Table 1, the sum of £100 invested in equities in 1925 with all income reinvested would be worth £500 in real terms in 1974. This conclusion – as it relates to past experience – cannot be over-emphasized: in comparing fixed-interest securities and equities many people think only of the income on the former (and neglect the loss of capital under inflation), while they think only of the capital values of equities (and neglect the income).

The fluctuations in equity values have meant, of course, that there are short periods over which the investor could lose quite heavily. A lump sum invested in 1965, for example, even with reinvested income would have lost 30 per cent of its real value by 1974, a negative annual return of 2·9 per cent – only half a percentage point less than if the money had been put in the Post Office.

My calculations for equities have assumed, in effect, that the investor bought shares at random and in sufficient number to ensure that his portfolio moved in line with the market average. It would, of course, be possible to do better or worse than the average and probably many private investors have done worse by delaying purchases until the index was well along its upward cycle and selling out in desperation near the trough. Others will have hung on through the ups and downs and achieved near the average, while a few will have got their timing and their share selection right and surpassed it.

Managed funds

A solution to this problem is to entrust your investment to pro-

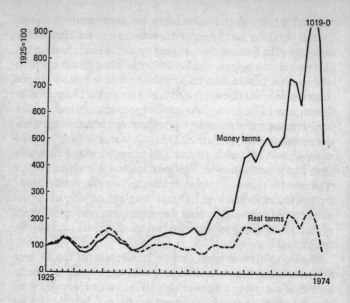

Chart 1: Ordinary Share Prices in Money and Real Terms, 1925–74

SOURCE: see Appendix I.

fessional management, but it is legitimate to inquire just what the performance record of managed investment is. There are many alternatives: investment trusts, unit trusts, offshore funds and various kinds of bonds, as well as a number of insurance-based investment vehicles. I found when I started the research for this book that there is a quite remarkable absence of systematic long-term comparative analysis of the net yields on managed funds compared with other kinds of investment. This is partly because the managed-funds industry has grown and changed out of all recognition in the post-war period, so that long-term comparisons with other types of investment are either difficult or impossible. The popularity of unit trusts in particular grew fast in the 1960s. In 1959 there were about half a million holdings in unit trusts, worth £200 million. By 1970 there were 2·4 million holdings, worth £1,400 million, although the number of holdings has levelled off since then.

Unit trusts invest funds subscribed by unit-holders in portfolios of ordinary shares and other securities; each unit-holder has a share in the value of the portfolio as a whole in proportion to the number of units he holds. The management deducts a percentage from funds subscribed as an initial charge and also levies an annual management charge. In addition, like any broker, it charges what is in effect commission for re-purchasing units. Unit trusts pay capital gains tax at a concessionary rate of 15 per cent. This gives them an advantage over the private direct investor, but at present this is not an effective advantage over inactive or small investors since capital gains tax is not payable on the first £500 of annual sales, or if annual gains do not exceed £50. So the investor who chooses to work through unit trusts pays additional charges (limited by government regulations to a maximum of 13·25 per cent of the value of units over a twenty-year period) but the administration of his investment is carried out for him and he can if he wishes choose trusts to maximize income or growth or, through specialized funds, to cater for his particular investment inclinations.

Such information as is available suggests that far more important than deciding between direct investment and unit trusts is the selection of the trust itself. Certainly professional management is not the way to certain riches. In 1974, of the 316 trusts monitored by *Money Management and Unit Holder*, all but seventeen managed to do better than the Financial Times Index, which fell in that year by 53 per cent. The two largest unit-trust groups, with fifteen and twenty trusts respectively, managed to beat the index by only 13 and 14 percentage points; however, the best performers among the major groups, Drayton and Slater-Walker, managed to beat it by 33 and 29 percentage points respectively. In the longer term it does appear that, *on average*, unit trusts outperform the Financial Times Index. Comparisons published in *Planned Savings* indicate that 89 per cent of unit trusts did better than the index over the ten years 1963–74.

The best-managed general unit trusts are probably the simplest and best way of investing in equities for the small saver. Some of the specialized unit trusts also offer a convenient means of investing overseas, which is something the investor should consider doing. Overseas investment in equities is not only difficult for the amateur investor because of the problem of obtaining sufficient information about foreign-based companies, it is also more costly and complicated because foreign exchange to purchase shares is available only from an investment pool on which a premium (the dollar premium) is payable.

The primary reason for investing overseas is to hedge against the possibility or, as I believe, the probability that the UK economy will continue to perform less well than that of some other countries. Some countries, like France and the United States, have faced fewer economic and social problems than Britain in the past few decades; others, such as Brazil (despite heavy inflation), Spain and some countries in the Far East, have also been able to grow more rapidly through a combination of liberal economic policies and favourable circumstances; others still, such as Switzerland and Germany, have pursued sounder monetary policies and their currencies have steadily appreciated against the pound. Some stake in the more rapid growth overseas and a hedge against continued depreciation of sterling can be obtained by investing in British companies with high overseas earnings, but this can also be achieved by investing in some unit trusts. I am not aware, however, of any satisfactory research on the relative performance of domestic and overseas unit trusts. More direct methods, such as taking out insurance policies denominated in Swiss Francs, are denied to UK residents by exchange-control regulations.

There are several other vehicles available for investing in equities (for instance, investment trusts) and many other types of financial asset besides those considered here, such as annuities, property bonds and equity-linked insurance and 'mixed asset' bonds. Although offering tax or technical advantages, which often carry with them disadvantages, these different vehicles are all based upon or analogous to either fixed-interest and equity securities or the real assets discussed in the next chapter, and do not merit detailed discussion in a general survey of this sort.[1] The only other financial asset which does require discussion is assurance.

Life assurance

Most insurance has nothing to do with saving, but endowment *assurance*, which guarantees a capital sum at a fixed future date with life cover in the event of death in the meantime, is an important means of saving. Its importance derives from the fact that tax relief at the rate of 16·5 per cent, subject to certain conditions, is given on the premiums paid.[2] This is in effect a form of fixed-interest investment, and it has offered a very poor return since the war as inflation has eroded the real value of the capital sum assured. However, with-profits policies, which carry bonuses which vary according to the performance of the insurance companies' life fund in which the premiums are invested, offer a much better return.

Assurance is only suitable for long-term investment, because tax relief is available only for policies having a term of at least ten

1. Premium bonds are really a form of gambling and must give pleasure to many people as such, but cannot be seriously regarded as an investment.

2. Somewhat higher relief is given where the total premiums do not exceed £20. The amount on which relief is given may not exceed one sixth of taxable income. There are a number of detailed provisions to prevent the use of insurance for tax avoidance. The insurance companies themselves also receive favourable tax treatment.

years, and because of the heavy cost of cashing in a policy before the full term. On a typical ten-year endowment policy without profits, surrender values after five years would be only about one third of the sum insured, even though half the premiums had been paid. With-profits policy-holders would fare better than this, because the annual bonuses declared are normally added to the surrender value of the policy. Even so, premature surrender of a with-profits policy involves some loss, if not the whole loss of the terminal bonus. This bonus is designed to give the policy-holder a share in the capital appreciation of the life fund. It could amount to as much as 70 per cent of the basic sum assured on a twenty-five year policy terminating in 1974.

The investor who takes out a with-profits endowment assurance is in effect buying shares in a managed fund in much the same way as he would if he subscribed a regular fixed sum to a unit trust. The Standard Life Company whose financial experience is used to illustrate this section have, according to their 1973 balance sheet, 30 per cent of their fixed assets in fixed-interest securities, 18 per cent in mortgages, deposits and loans, 41 per cent in equities and 11 per cent in property. There are very great differences between the performances of life funds and past experience indicates that the best life companies offer after-tax real returns which compare very favourably with any other form of paper asset, while the worst offer negative real returns. The number of companies which do offer very favourable returns is, however, very limited.

The *Economist* publishes a table each year giving the results achieved on with-profit assurance policies of various companies. The 1974 table gives the amounts payable in that year on policies of £50 annual premium taken out by a man aged twenty-nine at normal rates. For a twenty-five-year endowment policy started in 1949 and maturing in 1974 the total sum paid by forty-two companies varied from £2,119 to £3,477. Only four companies paid more than £3,000 and only eleven more than £2,750. The Standard Life was one of the top three; indeed, it has been in the top three every year since the surveys began in 1950. Scottish Widows is another company with a consistently good record. Both companies are mutual companies; that is to say, there are no shareholders and all profits are divided among participating policy-holders. Many other mutual companies were less success-

	Money return	Average annual increase in consumer prices	Average annual real increase (decrease)	
			Assurance	Industrial shares
10 year term (1964–74)	8·50	6·00	2·50	(1·75)
15 year term (1959–74)	8·75	5·50	3·25	0
20 year term (1954–74)	8·25	5·00	3·25	2·75
25 year term (1950–74)	8·00	5·00	3·00	3·26
30 year term (1944–74)	7·75	5·00	2·75	2·50

Table 3: 'Best' Achieved Net-of-Tax Real and Money Rates of Return on Endowment Assurance Policies Maturing in 1974

(Calculations are based upon actual Standard Life with-profits endowment policies maturing in 1974. The policies are for a man aged 30–31 at commencement paying a premium of £10 per month. This premium would give an initial sum assured of £1150 for the 10-year term, rising to £3300 for the 30-year term. Tax relief on the premiums is allowed for throughout. The returns are calculated to the nearest ¼ per cent. It should be emphasized that these returns are among the best and average returns are much lower.)

SOURCE: Information supplied by the Standard Life Assurance Company. Inflation rates were calculated from Appendix II, and the real returns on industrial shares are from the same sources as Table 1.

ful, however, and the superior results of these two companies must be attributed primarily to their underwriting and their investment policy.

I have selected Standard Life results for more detailed analysis in Table 3. It can be seen in this particular comparison, which ends in a period when stock-market prices were depressed, that the real returns on this company's policies were actually generally superior to those which could have been earned by investing in a representative index of equity shares. In the two shorter periods insurance performed very much better than the share index. This is because the sum assured and the annual bonuses are determined by the income of the life fund and are not affected by changes in its capital value. Thus, a stock-market crash will affect terminal bonuses (although even there the effects are damped down by the way this is calculated) and it may affect surrender values for policies encashed prematurely. This happened in 1974 when most companies revised surrender-values downwards, but stock-market fluctuations do not affect the sum assured or the accrued bonuses.

In comparing the return on insurance policies with that on other investments it should be remembered that the policy-holder is benefiting from life cover. With the best insurance companies this is, in effect, paid for by the tax concession.

This protection against sudden loss of capital values is, of course, bought at the cost of illiquidity, since policies cannot be surrendered prematurely without loss. However, the effects of this are to some extent mitigated by the fact that it is usually possible to borrow against surrender-values from the insurance company, often at very favourable rates of interest.

Insurance has one other advantage as a form of investment, the psychological one that the need to maintain insurance cover and the high penalties of premature surrender do help the average investor to keep on saving regularly, which he might find difficult to do in other ways.

The future outlook for paper assets

In the future, in which rising taxation, slower and perhaps more volatile economic growth, and continued but fluctuating rates of inflation are the principal features, the outlook for any form of investment is hardly bright.

No form of fixed-interest or interest-bearing deposit is likely to offer a real rate of return for the ordinary investor in the medium or long term. Interest rates will probably fluctuate about an upward-sloping trend, and this means that building society shares, and probably bank deposits and short-term bonds, will continue to offer much better returns than long-dated securities. As the rate at which the value of money declines speeds up, cash management – that is, keeping non-interest-bearing balances to a minimum – will be more and more important. I have emphasized elsewhere the uncertainties of the future and the importance of hedging against them. The question, therefore, arises: how to hedge against the possibility of *declining* interest rates ? Although as a sustained development this possibility does seem slight, interest rates will, in the short run, fall as well as rise and it is not totally inconceivable that interest rates could fall semi-permanently. There are, however, in my opinion better ways of hedging against this than buying gilts or debentures. One way is through equities which, in most though not all circumstances, would also benefit from a fall in interest rates; another is through endowment assurance. If the value of money falls faster than expected, any form of fixed-interest investment will rapidly become worthless and this means that now even gilt-edged securities are a high-risk long-term investment.

Equities, both on their past record and in economic logic, look a much better long-term bet in the conditions envisaged for the future than any form of interest-bearing deposit or security. Even so it is doubtful, under conditions of moderate but, by historical standards, still rapid inflation, that the average appreciation in share values will significantly exceed the increase in prices. History in Brazil and Germany suggests that under hyper-inflation equity prices at first keep pace with the price-level, but then fall behind and eventually far behind. The lesson here would be to switch out of equities as soon as it was clear that the price-level could not be controlled. The outlook for equities would, of course, be better in the United Kingdom if price and dividend controls were removed, but this does not seem likely and I expect them to become permanent in some form. The existence of controls will probably ensure that average historical rates of real return on equities will not be maintained. The decline in the importance of the profit motive, and other social and economic changes that are to be described in more detail in Part II, will also depress the returns on equities.

Continuing controls over corporate financial performance combined with these other changes can be expected to continue to have interesting effects upon the performance of different types of public-company shares. The earnings of the largest companies are more stable and the yields correspondingly lower than for smaller companies. This should mean that there will be more scope for capital gains in the so-called 'second line' shares of smaller public companies and, perhaps, less risk to be borne in the shares of larger companies. To this extent the shares of the larger companies will become more and more like fixed-interest securities, but with dividends that bear some, albeit elastic, relationship to the price-level. This is not to say that earnings will not fluctuate quite sharply when events occur that are outside the control of companies or government – as happened when increased oil prices boosted the profits of oil companies in 1973–4. As I shall point out later on, some industries may well have better profit prospects than others, so that share selection, where this is not delegated to professional management, will still be as important in the future as it has been in the past.

The outlook for insurance as an investment will be dominated by the tax treatment accorded to it, but I see no reason why the present favourable treatment will not be continued; indeed, the net of tax advantages may improve as taxes rise. Because of the importance of good investment policy the choice of company will remain critical. Their need to invest to meet fixed obligations means that insurance companies are heavy investors in fixed-interest securities. With-profit policy-holders would benefit from any sustained improvement in prices and interest rates, and the real value of sums assured would actually increase if the price-level fell. This is why endowment insurance is a hedge against the unlikely possibility of a sustained decline in prices and interest rates.

Indexation

One major development which would radically affect the conclusions drawn here would be for the government to introduce indexation on a large scale. Indexation means the introduction of automatic links between monetary obligations and the price-level. In practice this would mean, for example, that the principal of a long-term loan would be increased in line with the cost of living or some other index so that its real value would be maintained. If inflation is not kept under control indexation is a very real possibility, since without it the credit mechanism and the government's ability to borrow will be steadily eroded. Only the government would initiate indexation of savings, although escalator clauses are already common in many other kinds of contract – for example, wages and commercial agreements in both public and private sectors – but private financial institutions would be obliged to follow. Taxes would probably also be indexed. All this has been done in Brazil.

We may be sure that the government will be reluctant to introduce indexation since it would heavily increase the real cost of borrowing, but it is certain to do so if inflation continues at anything around recent peak levels. Many economists believe that indexation would contribute to the control of inflation, though others think it would make matters worse. I do not think that in itself the indexation of debt will make much difference to the rate of inflation, but it will reduce some of the hardship and unite the interests of both borrowers and lenders in doing something about controlling it.

In fact, the government has already announced the introduction of two indexed savings media in the summer of 1975. The first, to be introduced on 2 June, are Retirement Certificates, available only to persons of pensionable age. Lenders can buy certificates in units of £10 and up to a maximum of £500. All payments on the certificates are tax free. For five years the value of the certificates will be increased in line with the cost of living, and at the end of the fifth year a bonus of 4 per cent on the purchase price will be added. Thus the annual after-tax real return will exceed zero by whatever the real value of the 4-per-cent bonus is, calculated as a compound return on the purchase price over five years. This will not be much – even if prices did not rise at all it would be much less than 1 per cent – but even a zero real return compares favourably with a *negative* return of 3·5 per cent on National Savings and much lower returns on consols in the last ten years. To give a zero real return over the five years 1969–74 the government would have had to pay 10 per cent free of tax per annum on savings deposits or certificates.

The second indexed savings scheme will replace the second Save-as-You-Earn issue. It provides for monthly contributions of a minimum of £4 and a maximum of £20 which can be withdrawn at the end of either five or seven years, each payment having been increased in line with consumer prices. If the investor delays withdrawal until the seventh year he is also paid a bonus equal to two monthly payments.

Although neither scheme is apparently intended by the government to offer a real after-tax return of more than 1 per cent, they must be regarded as very good buys compared with the terms of other post-war borrowings, and they have at least a chance of offering a better return than any other form of paper asset. They are also the only paper asset which provides guaranteed protection of the real value of your capital even under hyper-inflation and should, therefore, be taken up by all except the most optimistic savers. There are many signs, including the publication of a growing number of papers by government statisticians on the practical implications of indexation, that the establishment is preparing itself to accommodate indexed government debt, first for more forms of national savings and later on for other types of government borrowing. It would take several years for indexation to become widespread but I believe it will come, and surprisingly soon.

Assuming house prices continue to rise at least in line with the cost of living, there is one way in which an elderly person can obtain an income that will rise as inflation continues: participating in a home income plan. Under these home plans, the investor takes out a mortgage on his house from a life insurance company. The company allows him to use the mortgage money to buy an annuity which provides him with an income. The annuity can be increased from time to time by effecting additional mortgages as the value of the house increases. On the death of the investor, or on that of his wife if she survives him, the mortgage is repaid by a life assurance policy incorporated in the plan. The income yielded by the scheme is not as high as on a conventional annuity, because the annuity is paid net of the mortgage-interest payments (on which, however, tax relief is available) and life-assurance premiums, but it does greatly reduce the risk that investment income will be irretrievably eroded by inflation, and protects the investor's ability to leave his house to his family after his death. There are several permutations of these plans, including, I understand, one of superb ingenuity and complexity which links both the annuity payments and the interest payments to units in a unit trust. Professional advice from a good independent insurance broker should be taken before taking the important step of participating in a home income plan.

4. Gold

The value of gold

Virtually all general bookshops in the United States offer a choice of manuals on how to become rich. These books are enormously popular and several have sold more than a million copies, evidence that they have at least gone some way towards fulfilling their function, for their authors if not their readers. The very absence, or at least muted existence, of such books in Britain tells us something of the difference between the social basis of capitalism in the two countries. Can you imagine, for example, how one title that appeared in the US in mid-1973, *How to Make Money Fast by Speculating in Distressed Property* would be received in this country? Many of these books are technical guides to speculation, but among the most popular recently have been several that are simply apocalyptic in their outlook. They are without exception based upon the view that our economic difficulties are the result of governments' printing too much paper money and that violent fluctuations in output and employment will continue until sound money is restored and market forces are allowed to operate freely.

Probably the best and certainly one of the most successful writers in this school is Harry Browne, who correctly forecast the 1971 devaluation of the US dollar in a book entitled *How You Can Profit from the Coming Devaluation* (1970). He followed this book with another, *You Can Profit from the Monetary Crisis* (1974). Harry D. Schultz is another writer with a long run of successful books on personal protection against inflation with what is, in effect, the same theme as Browne's: 'How to step around government mismanagement . . . and still come out ahead.' The principal means recommended for achieving this ambitious objective is to invest in gold, which Schultz considers 'an ideal hedge against monetary instability in times of crisis'. Browne believes that gold is 'the best long-term store of value', and indeed dismisses all other forms of investment except silver and foreign currencies with a high gold backing.

Gold has a very long history. In our childhood it glistens back at us from the distant past in stories about the Egyptians, the Greeks and the Romans, and later on in tales about pirates and the Wild West of America. Today, as adults, we know that gold is still as valuable as ever, although most of us never see any except in rings and jewellery. Why is gold so valuable and what magic property has it that gives these writers the confidence to assert that it is the ideal and only safe thing in which to invest?

Gold is, of course, a beautiful colour, either on its own or blended with silver or platinum; it has a pleasing texture, is non-toxic, does not tarnish and is impervious to almost all corrosive agents including acids. It is an excellent conductor of electricity. One ounce of gold can be beaten into a sheet a hundred feet square or drawn continuously into fifty miles of thin wire. It is also very 'dense': twice as heavy as lead and the heaviest of all materials except tungsten; a cubic foot of gold weighs well over half a ton. These qualities make it very useful and desirable, but what makes it so valuable is that it is also extremely scarce.

Chart 2 illustrates how scarce gold is. It is estimated that some 80,000 metric tons have been extracted from the earth since history began. I do not suppose this estimate is at all accurate for earlier years, but it does not matter too much since most of it – 70,000 tons – is calculated to have been mined since 1850. Anyway, the whole lot could be melted into bars and stacked in a block about 53 feet square. This would fit easily into the auditorium of the Royal Festival Hall in London, or the bars could all be loaded into a medium-sized oil-tanker. The value of the world's gold at 1974 prices would be $450 billion, which sounds a lot, but if it were divided equally among the world's population there would be only a three-quarter-ounce bar each, worth about $120 or £50.

Supply and demand

The value of gold is not too difficult to understand; but it would not be a good store of value if the supply were to increase suddenly,

67

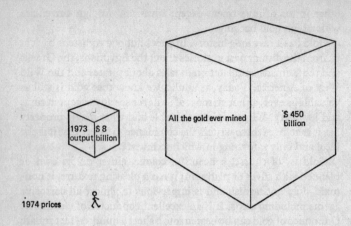

1973
output | $ 8
billion

All the gold ever mined | $ 450
billion

1974 prices

Chart 2: The World Gold Stock and 1973 Mining Production (1974 prices)

or if large stocks were liquidated suddenly, or if the demand for gold fell heavily for some reason. All these things could adversely affect the price of gold.

The total world production of gold in 1973 was of the order of 1,500 tons. On Chart 2, 1973 output is shown as a cube on the same scale as the gold stock; it is relatively small and amounts to about 1·8 per cent of the total. This happens to be close to the annual rate at which world population is growing. The mining of gold is carried on in many countries, but South Africa is far ahead of the rest, and, with the USSR, accounts for nearly 82 per cent of world output, as Table 4 shows. Not much is known about gold pro-

Metric tons

	1968	1973	% of total
South Africa	969·4	852·3	56·9
USSR	304·2	370·6	24·7
Canada	83·6	60·0	4·0
USA	46·0	36·2	2·4
Ghana	22·6	25·0	1·7
Papua/New Guinea	0·8	20·3	1·4
Australia	24·3	18·4	1·2
Philippines	16·4	18·1	1·2
Rhodesia	15·5	15·6	1·0
Japan	7·0	10·4	0·7
Other	67·8	72·2	4·8
Total	1,557·6	1,499·1	100·0

SOURCE: *Gold 1974*, Consolidated Goldfields Limited

Table 4: World Gold Production in 1968 and 1973 by Country

duction in Russia. Even the output figure in the table is an estimate, but it is believed that Russia has considerable unexploited reserves. This cannot be said for South Africa where costs are rising sharply as the existing mines are being worked out. The ERPM Mine on the East Rand, for example, is now over 11,000 feet deep (the workings follow a downward-sloping seam) and the temperatures at that depth are so high that refrigeration is necessary.

The supply of gold depends both upon the availability of reserves and the profitability of exploiting them, and this in turn depends upon the price of gold. This does not carry us very far in itself, but at least there seems to be general agreement among the experts that a new gold rush elsewhere in the world is unlikely. It takes many years to develop a new mine and most surface gold has long since gone, so any rapid increase in the supply of newly mined gold is also unlikely. It seems probable that Russia's share of world output will increase and South Africa's tend to decline. What happens among the smaller producers is not likely to affect the price very much. This, at least, is what the experts say, and it sounds plausible. The recent increase in gold prices, which I shall come to later on, will help to keep gold production up, but production outside the Communist countries has not increased at all in the last decade or so.

Table 5, which breaks down the 1973 supply position (outside the Communist countries) into its component parts, shows that these countries are heavy net sellers of gold to the West. This is the first big destabilizing threat to gold. The Communist countries have in the past twenty years been mainly net sellers of gold to the West on a fluctuating annual scale varying from 60 tons to 489 tons, although between 1966 and 1969 they were net buyers. In the last four years they have been growing sellers, but it seems unlikely that the Russians would wish to depress the gold price by unloading their substantial stocks on to the world market.

The international monetary system

Table 5 also shows that in 1973 world monetary authorities were net sellers of gold to the private sector. The amount was, in fact, the smallest net amount sold or bought by monetary authorities since the Second World War. Until 1965 monetary authorities were consistent net buyers of gold, but since then they have tended to be larger net sellers than buyers. Since about half of the world's gold stock lies in the vaults of central banks and other financial

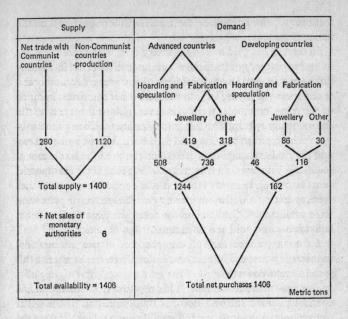

Supply		Demand	
Net trade with Communist countries	Non-Communist countries production	Advanced countries	Developing countries

Advanced countries:
Hoarding and speculation — Fabrication (Jewellery 419, Other 318)

Developing countries:
Hoarding and speculation — Fabrication (Jewellery 86, Other 30)

280   1120

419   318   86   30

508   736   46   116

Total supply = 1400   1244   162

+ Net sales of monetary authorities   6

Total availability = 1406   Total net purchases 1406

Metric tons

SOURCE: *Gold 1974*, Consolidated Goldfields Limited.

Table 5: Non-Communist World Private Sector Supply and Demand for Gold, 1973

institutions, the attitude of these authorities to gold will have a major effect upon its price.

In the USSR gold has no monetary role, in the sense that the domestic currency or its foreign-exchange value is not in any way linked to gold, and Russia's gold reserves are regarded simply as a useful means of paying for imports from other countries. In much of the non-Communist world, however, gold still plays a role in the monetary system. The full gold standard which required convertibility between currency and gold both at home and overseas, and the gold exchange standard which required the settlement of payments between countries in gold, have long since disappeared (see Chapter 6). In most of the post-war period Western countries were operating a dollar-standard by which exchange rates were fixed against the US dollar and the dollar was, nominally at least, convertible into gold at a fixed rate of $35 an ounce.

I cannot go into the full complexities of the international monetary system and its post-war history here, but in essence this system broke down because of the growing weakness of the dollar in foreign-exchange markets. This resulted from excessive US spending abroad and was not met by devaluation of the dollar against gold. As a result, the US steadily lost gold to the rest of the world; between 1949 and 1965, for example, its gold reserves fell from over 650 million to under 400 million ounces. In December 1971 the US formally suspended gold payments and raised the price of gold to $38 per ounce. Several major currencies were floated against the dollar at the same time; that is to say, fixed exchange rates were abandoned and currencies were allowed to find their own level against the dollar (with some intervention in the market from central banks). The dollar was again devalued against gold, to $42·22 per ounce, in February 1973.

Until 1968 the world price of gold had been kept to $35 an ounce, the official rate; but in that year a two-tier system was introduced, under which central banks agreed to settle payments among themselves at the official, monetary rate, while a free market in non-monetary gold was introduced, in which central banks agreed not to buy and sell (this agreement has since expired).

Until 1972 the free-market price did not stray very far from the official price, but since then it has shot up, as confidence in the stability of the world monetary system has diminished in the face of the oil crisis and the acceleration in world inflation.

Unsurprisingly, in view of the wide discrepancy between the free-market gold price and the official price, central banks have been reluctant to make settlements in gold and the role of the metal in the international monetary system is now more apparent than real.

The outlook for gold

The US authorities have declared their intention to 'demonetize' gold altogether, so that it will become a free-market commodity like silver or any other. As an apparent step towards this, US citizens have since January 1975 been allowed to hold gold in bullion or any other form, and the US Treasury auctioned 2 million ounces of gold at that time to prevent an increase in the free-market price. This was successful and reinforced a tendency for the gold price to soften, following growing fears of a world recession. If the US or other monetary authorities continue to sell gold on the free market, this will obviously have a depressing effect upon the gold price.

There are considerable differences among the advanced countries about the future monetary role of gold, but it seems highly unlikely that the gold standard will be restored, or even that gold will play a major part in any disciplinary mechanism on the growth of the world monetary supply or in the determination of exchange rates. Not only would such a move now be regarded as an unacceptable restriction on the freedom of governments to pursue independent economic policies, but it would, through an increase in the official price of gold, greatly benefit South Africa and the USSR as the two major gold stockholders and producers. This would be politically unacceptable in the present climate. Indeed, although there are signs that some means of bringing the official and free-market gold prices nearer each other will be found, in my opinion the restoration of the full monetary role of gold is so much out of keeping with the long-term economic and political trends described in Part II of this book that it will never happen. Governments will, however, clearly have no interest in forcing down the value of their gold stocks by unloading gold on to the free market, and it seems probable that it will take a very long time indeed for gold to become demonetized altogether.

Nor does it seem likely, in a period in which the general level of prices is expected to continue to rise rapidly, that the demand for gold for private investment and speculation will fall away permanently. The demand for gold for jewellery and, to a lesser extent, for industrial purposes is fairly sensitive to the gold price – the demand for gold for jewellery in particular fell away sharply in 1973 as the price of gold rose – but this demand helps to support the gold price. One factor which could have an important effect upon gold prices is the attitude of the oil-producing countries. So far they have not chosen to increase their holdings of gold in line with their new role in the world economy. Should they do so, this would tend to push up the gold price.

In the very long run, gold has maintained its value in terms of real purchasing power. At the end of 1974 *The Times* Business Diary carried a story to the effect that gold prices have risen some twenty times since 1933 – remarkably close to the recorded price-increases of such basic foodstuffs as milk and eggs over the same period. Nevertheless, speculation and changes in the supply and demand for gold and in the intervention of governments in the market place have resulted in violent fluctuations in the gold price over the same time. In a period of cyclical stag-flation such as we expect, fluctuations in the gold price will continue. Gold purchased in 1925 would have been worth nearly double in real terms in 1974 (that is, allowing for the decline in the value of money), but if the purchaser had sold out in 1965 he would only just have maintained the real value of his investment. If he had bought in 1939 and sold in 1955 he would have lost over 30 per cent in real terms. The average annual price of gold on the London Market between 1925 and 1974 is given in Appendix II. Appendix III, which gives monthly gold prices since 1968, shows that even in this favourable period fluctuations have been considerable.

How to invest in gold

Gold has not provided a perfect solution to the problem of personal investment in the past, nor is it likely to in the future, but I think it should have some place in the security-conscious investor's portfolio. This is simply because gold offers the best liquid (i.e., readily realizable) protection against rapid depreciation of the currency.

There are three forms in which the individual can invest in gold: jewellery and other gold objects, coins, and gold-mining shares. UK residents are not allowed to hold or to buy and sell gold bullion unless they are authorized dealers in gold or approved industrial users. Jewellery is an expensive way of buying gold, since you will probably have to pay at least twice the value of the gold content; that is, the *premium* over the value of the gold in the article may be 100 per cent or more. This is not to say that you should not buy jewellery if you like it. Some fine pieces of antique jewellery have also appreciated rapidly but they are more properly regarded as investments in antiques or art rather than in gold.

There are no restrictions, at the time of writing, on the ownership of gold coins. The buyer should beware of modern commemorative gold coins which are often sold at a very high premium and are not likely to acquire great scarcity value for a very long time. Other gold coins no longer in circulation, such as old sovereigns or Queen Elizabeth sovereigns, have a lower but still fairly high premium (55 and 29 per cent respectively recently, but the premia fluctuate with supply and demand). Coins of this sort must be regarded as mixed investments, in scarce coins as such, and in gold. Some foreign gold coins, such as French 20-Franc pieces, Italian 20-Lire pieces or US $20 pieces, which are greatly in demand in their countries of origin, may have higher premia still.

At the time of writing, Krugerrands from South Africa have the lowest premium over their gold content (about 3 per cent, but it has been 20 per cent) and if dealt through a reputable dealer in some quantity are the best way of buying or selling gold for the ordinary person. These coins have a low premium because they are legal tender in South Africa and are available in great quantity: the South African Mint struck 853,000 of them in 1973 alone. The special advantage of gold coins is that they are compact and portable and easily stored. The price of Krugerrands is given daily in the financial press. They could be bought (in quantity) for £77·25 each and sold for £75·25 each on 6 February 1975, so that a small pile of six would be worth £450. At present, capital gains tax is not payable on the proceeds of the sale of Krugerrands or any other coin which is legal tender. Some of the apocalyptic writers referred to have pointed out that in the event of a total collapse of the currency you could actually go out and buy things with gold coins, but change would be a problem.

At first sight gold-mining shares appear to be an ideal investment since, as a group, mining-share prices tend to move with the price of gold but, unlike gold, shares yield an income. In fact, however, the choice of shares is virtually limited to South African mines where profitability is not expected to be very buoyant and where political risks are high. Mining shares are also subject to the dollar premium which gears down the benefit which the investor receives from an increase in the price of gold. Certainly, the small investor would be best-advised to buy gold-mining shares through a unit trust to minimize the risks from the impact of labour or other troubles, such as flooding, which can affect any single company.[1] One historical feature of mining shares which is useful is that they tend to move in the opposite direction from other equity shares, so that they provide a useful hedge element in any portfolio of equity shares.

Silver

Gold is not, of course, the only precious metal. Platinum is also valuable though not so easily tradeable. Silver is the metal second to gold, and it has some advantages: it is demonetized, and governments no longer find it attractive to tamper with the price or to place restrictions on holding, buying and selling it. Silver also has very great (and growing) industrial applications. There is, however, a lot of silver about, and, at $4.50 an ounce compared with $188 for gold, you need much more of it as a store of value. The experts say that the silver price is vulnerable to declining industrial

1. By arranging what are called 'back-to-back' financing arrangements, unit trusts are also able to minimize the adverse effects of the dollar premium on foreign shares.

activity which is reducing the industrial demand for it. In the long run, however, it's bound to be better than cash.

5. Savings and Investment: II

Real versus paper assets

The purpose of this chapter is to inquire whether or not better returns might be available on real as distinct from paper assets. In its usual form the distinction between 'real' and 'paper' is not clear-cut, because many paper assets are in fact titles to real assets such as buildings and machinery and the income these generate. It is more useful, perhaps, to distinguish between the following: *pure paper assets* (cash, fixed-interest securities, and titles to deposits of various kinds); *commercial paper assets* (such as equities and property bonds), which are paper titles to ownership of bundles of organization and sometimes qualified and indirect titles to commodities and fixed assets which generate income; and *personal real assets* (such as houses and furniture), which can be directly, or, as with a mortgaged property, indirectly, owned.

Commercial paper assets were dealt with in Chapter 3, where I showed that, because their yields to the holder tend to increase in money terms as the value of money falls, they have proved better investments than pure paper assets. Gold, which is a real asset and can be held personally in the form of coins and jewellery, or through equity shares in mining companies, was discussed in Chapter 4. Hoarding of consumption goods, which are also real assets, was examined in Chapter 2.

Although, in the long run, commercial paper assets have proved capable of offering a real return on savings (that is, they have preserved the value of capital and produced some net-of-tax income or growth in capital), these returns have tended to decline with the post-war acceleration in inflation. With the prospect of slow economic growth, continuing inflation and controls over profits, it seems likely that these returns will not improve and might well continue to deteriorate. The introduction of indexation would require some re-ordering of the merits of different types of paper assets in favour of pure paper assets, but it is difficult to see how it could result in a major increase in real after-tax returns.

This sombre conclusion leaves us with personal real assets. Here, future as well as past prospects are a little brighter. This may have something to do with the nature of the market for personal assets and it could also reflect changes that are going on in capital markets, which are described in Chapter 9. Abstract arguments are not, however, needed to explain why the prices of houses and antiques have risen rapidly in the long term. There is a continuing pressure of demand for houses as population increases and living standards rise. This demand has been heightened by the subsidization of house-purchase through the tax system and through the relatively easy availability of credit. On the supply side, the amount of land available is more or less fixed and the costs of construction, this being a labour-intensive activity, have risen rapidly. Government controls on housing through rent, planning and other restrictions have also limited the supply of housing. Similarly with antiques: the supply of genuine antiques from any given period in the past is also fixed, and the cost of modern substitutes, again because of rising labour costs, has risen rapidly. The pressure of demand for antiques, like that for houses, is maintained not only by rising living-standards but also by a widening belief in their qualities as hedges against inflation.

The assessment of the actual returns enjoyed on personal real assets in the past and in the future is not easy, for four reasons. First, virtually no systematic statistical information is available on the prices at which personal real assets change hands, with the exception of dwelling houses. Second, these assets do not merely change (generally appreciate) in value, they also yield a use-value which is often difficult to express in money terms. Third, in general the appreciation on personal real assets is tax-free for the ordinary taxpayer, although in certain circumstances sales of assets can result in liability for capital gains tax. The reader should seek professional advice on this question, but, briefly, the tax position on personal property is as follows. The proceeds of the sale of owner-occupied dwellings are not liable to capital gains tax at all unless income-tax relief has been claimed in respect of their use for business or professional purposes. Capital gains from the sale of 'chattels', which covers the other personal real assets considered in this chapter, are not liable for tax unless their value exceeds £1,000, and even then reliefs reduce the rate of tax to quite low levels on modest items. The fourth general problem about the returns on personal real assets is that, compared with pure paper assets or commercial paper assets (except insurance), they are illiquid, and quite high transaction costs are incurred in buying and selling them.

The rest of this chapter looks in more detail at two kinds of personal real assets – property and antique furniture. These are two of the most attractive and familiar assets in which the ordinary person invests. There are many others, including old motor-cars, wines and liqueurs, works of art, glass, china, horses, carpets, books, jewellery and all sorts of old articles from clothes to Oxo tins, all with their own advantages and dangers and requiring varying amounts of capital and knowledge.

Property

Everyone knows that property has been a good investment in the past. The evidence supports this belief (see Table 1a, p. 48) but there is no readily available information of a systematic kind on house prices before 1939. From that date onwards in Table 1a the figures are based on the prices of houses financed by building societies. For the years before 1939 I have been obliged to make an informed guess. It would be wise, therefore, not to place much reliance upon the pre-war figures, which suggest that house prices rose in real terms by less than 10 per cent between 1925 and 1939. Since 1939, however, the rate of increase has been rising rapidly: from 2 per cent per annum between 1939 and 1955 to 2·7 per annum between 1955 and 1965 and 3·9 per cent per annum between 1965 and 1974. This continuing upward trend contrasts with the downward rate of return on all paper assets in the latter part of the period. The comparison is, moreover, understated for two reasons.

The first is that, in calculating the return on paper assets, income accruing was included, but the return on investment in property was simply taken to be the increase in market values. The owner-occupier would have lived in the house rent-free over the period, so the return to him should include an imputed rent less the costs of maintaining the structure of the house. This imputed rent is also a tax-free benefit and should be grossed up at the standard rate of tax to give a true comparison with the other investments considered. The return on property rented out to third parties would be lower, not only because the income would be taxed but also because controls on rented property affect the capital values of houses through their restrictions upon obtaining vacant possession.

The second reason why the figures in Table 1a understate the return on property compared with other assets is that, although the individual usually purchases paper assets for cash, he normally finances a house purchase by a loan. Although not generally at fixed interest, the interest on house-purchase loans is tax-deductible and the real after-tax interest-rate has been very low in the post-war period for standard-rate taxpayers. This method of financing greatly 'gears up' the return on the money invested in a house. In Table 1a I have assumed that the house-purchase was made with cash. Where the purchase was financed by a loan, the real returns on the actual cash outlay, after allowance for interest, would be very much higher.

The combined effect of these two factors is to raise the rate of return on house-purchase for the standard-rate taxpayer in the post-war period to astonishing levels. In the ten years 1964–74 the average discounted real after-tax rate of return on house-purchase was probably well in excess of 30 per cent per annum, even after transaction costs are allowed for.

It is very doubtful if the investor can expect returns of this order in the future, but for owner-occupied property there is every reason to suppose that returns will continue to be higher and more secure than those for other investments. Continuing inflation will ensure that the cost of building new houses will rise, and the pressure of demand for improved standards of accommodation and for house-purchase as a hedge against inflation will continue. This pressure will no doubt abate if economic growth remains slow, but it will not disappear. About one out of every two households are owner-occupiers and the withdrawal of tax incentives is politically unrealistic.

The main threat to house prices and the returns on house-purchase lies in the implications of inflation for financing these purchases. Increases in interest rates in 1973-4, even though they were negative rates, (that is, below the rise in the cost of living), placed a heavy burden upon borrowers, and further increases may be necessary if the building societies are to continue to attract funds if and when inflation pushes up the general level of interest rates. This would inevitably occur if building societies were obliged to follow the government in indexing deposits. For this reason it would be imprudent for house-buyers to over-borrow, as many of them have in the past, in the expectation that inflation will drastically reduce the real burden of interest and mortgage repayments. House-buyers whose incomes are not likely to keep pace with inflation will have to be particularly cautious. Indexation would not eliminate the attractions of house-purchase, since the overall return on owner-occupied property can be expected to be higher than the real rate of interest, but it would certainly reduce the rate of return on loan-financed property.

The recent withdrawal of tax relief on borrowing for the purchase of second homes and the continuing regulation of rents have greatly reduced the attractiveness of all forms of investment in property other than owner-occupation. These factors are also instrumental in reducing the pressure of demand on property in general. The returns on property are so superior to those on other forms of investment (and likely to continue so) that the purchase of a second home is still worth considering for the minority who are able to afford it. This acquisition could be made abroad. Every family has the right to apply for the foreign currency to purchase one property abroad. The pros and cons of foreign property-purchase are complex. *Against* are the high cost of the dollar premium payable on the necessary currency, the rising cost of visiting the property, and the political risks abroad. *For* are the lower absolute price of property, property taxes and rates in many countries abroad compared with Britain, the possibility of more rapid appreciation through better economic prospects abroad, and the probability of appreciation through exchange-rate changes against the pound sterling. The uncertainties are considerable but in my opinion overseas property-purchase, particularly within the EEC, is still an attractive proposition.

Antiques

Even less statistical information is readily available about the prices of antiques and works of art in the long term. The difficulties of compiling such information are great, since most sales and purchases are not available for public record and the articles concerned are, for the most part, hand-made and therefore unique. *The Times* newspaper and Sothebys the auctioneers did publish an index of prices for fine china, silver and other antiques for a few years, but this was discontinued in 1971. The only long-term series that I have been able to find relates to English furniture sold in the United States, and this information is the basis of the figures given in Table 1. This index, which I am told can also be taken as a very rough indication of price-movements in Britain, shows that antique-furniture prices fell quite sharply in real terms between 1925 and 1939 but that since then these prices have risen at about twice the rate of property prices.

Transaction costs for antiques are relatively high – perhaps as much as 20 per cent for sales at auction, plus transport costs, and 25 per cent or more for sales through a dealer. Furniture, in particular, is sensitive to heat and humidity, and all antiques require careful treatment if they are to be kept in good condition. For smaller articles security from theft is a problem – one which is almost totally absent with property or paper assets.

The yield on antiques is a subjective one and cannot be measured in money terms; but it is very real, nonetheless. Generally speaking it seems to be a good rule that if you do not consider the yield in pleasure from owning antiques to be very great you should not buy them. In other words, antiques should not be bought solely as an investment. There are good reasons for this. Fashion seems to play quite a large role in determining the price of antiques and works of art, and while I am writing here about things which can be bought for up to a few hundred pounds – I do not have the knowledge to presume to advise those who are able to invest thousands – there is still a risk that prices could fall.

If you invest in something which gives you pleasure to look at, or which you can use, if the price falls your pleasure will remain – if it is just an investment you will have lost so much more. But, in addition to this, if you do not get real and continuing pleasure from a painting or a piece of furniture it is probably either because you do not have the eye for art and workmanship and history or because the article is not a good one of its kind. You must cultivate the ability to distinguish good from bad, or you will soon make a mistake and pay much more than something is worth. Aesthetic taste is not a sufficient condition for successful investment in antiques and art but it is a necessary one – unless, that is, you have good professional advice. This you will not always have if you buy at auctions which are, on the whole, the cheapest places to buy.

In general, good antiques will continue to appreciate in the long term, and in my opinion the best examples provide an excellent means, probably the best means, of protecting small savings that are not expected to be needed for a very long time. The introduction of a wealth tax in the United Kingdom is not likely to affect unfavourably the prices of the sort of articles I am writing about here, and, if the long-term trend towards the redistribution of incomes continues as I expect, this will tend to increase rather than diminish the demand for the less expensive items.

Savings and investment summarized

Whilst the individual will need to retain some money in relatively liquid form in paper assets, my conclusion is that un-indexed deposits or fixed-interest securities of any kind are not a wise investment for the long-term saver. They are, at best, leaky buckets out of which the real value of savings will seep away. Insurance (with profits) and equity shares or trusts are the only paper assets which offer any prospect of protection against continued inflation; insurance also provides some hedge against the remote possibility that prices will stabilize in the foreseeable future. Equities are something of a gamble even in the long term, but they do offer the excitement of a gamble. None of these paper assets offers real protection against hyper-inflation; possibly not even against inflation at the rate experienced in 1974–5 if it should continue.

If inflation is not brought under control soon, then indexation of government, and eventually other, borrowings will be brought in, which will give protection to liquid assets and ease the problems of those who need an investment income. Investors should not be deterred by the apparently low return on indexed savings if they need to maintain access to their money. Even the pilot indexed schemes now being introduced by the government look good bets, and those with only a few hundred pounds to invest can probably do no better. If widespread indexation occurs, investment in equities should be reduced and narrowed to overseas shares in countries with relatively sound economies, gold-mining shares, and others whose earnings are likely to be exceptionally buoyant under inflation or which have very heavy backing in real assets and little indexed debt, such as some property companies. In the absence of indexation, gold is probably the best thing to hold under conditions of rapid inflation and where liquidity is required, but even gold is certainly not free of risk.

The safest and most satisfying protection for long-term investments is to be found only in personal real assets, including home-ownership and antiques. These are not easily realized without heavy loss in times of economic crisis, but means are available for obtaining income from an owner-occupied house by participating in home plans (see pages 64–5).

These recommendations do not cover some of the graver contingencies which could occur, but I do not believe it is very useful, or indeed socially desirable, for the individual to plan for chaos. Those who advocate the development of complete self-sufficiency to cater for the complete breakdown of the social and economic system are dreaming – in a dense populated island like Britain such efforts would be better devoted to taking lessons in unarmed combat. In the event of social breakdown it is unlikely that anyone would be left in peace to grow his own potatoes. Similarly, there is little point in recommending investments to cover the possibility of the rapid disappearance of what remains of the capitalist system, though if this is what you think will happen, equities are obviously the thing to get out of.

Finally, I have been primarily concerned in this and the two previous chapters with long-term investment. Interest rates and inflation rates and other economic variables will continue to fluctuate, and so will expectations about them and hence the prices of shares, securities and real assets, especially gold. These fluctuations will create opportunities for speculation on returns to trend for which, if they are correct, the long-term trends defined here will offer helpful guidance. I do not advise speculation, though, unless you have the taste and nerve for it and can afford to take losses when they occur.

Part II

Understanding the System

6. Inflation, Boom and Slump

World-wide inflation

Generally rising prices (inflation) in Britain are not in fact new: as measured by the consumer price-index, prices have risen every single year since 1944. Chart 3 shows that inflation since the Second World War has lasted very much longer than that which followed the First World War; the last three decades present a marked contrast to the experience of the earlier part of this century when prices remained relatively stable, or even declined, for long periods. I have not attempted to go farther back in time than this, but some economists claim to have established a fluctuating price level, gently rising but with periods of decline, going right back to the thirteenth century. Since the Second World War the *rate* of increase in prices, that is to say the annual increase over the previous year (Chart 4), has fluctuated around a downward trend from an immediate post-war peak of almost 10 per cent in 1951 to around 1 per cent in 1959–60. Between then and 1968 the rate of increase rose gently, and since 1968 it has been rising rapidly to reach, in 1974, the level of 16 per cent. In the first few months of 1975 prices were standing at a level some 20 per cent above that of a year previously: the biggest increase since 1915.

Even to a public long accustomed to rising prices, albeit at varying rates, increases of this order were a nasty, and for some a painful, shock. At 20 per cent per annum, prices would double in less than four years. The real value of savings, even invested in a building society at a tax-paid 7·5 per cent, the going rate at that time, would fall by almost two thirds in ten years. Worse still, for the first time it dawned upon more and more people in Britain that if prices could rise by 16 or 20 per cent in a year, they could rise by 40 per cent or 100 per cent or more, as had happened in Brazil and in Germany before the war. (The curve on Chart 3 looks like the trajectory of a space rocket.) Even at 16-per-cent

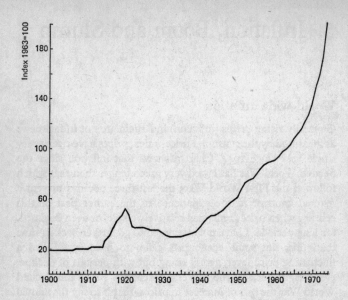

Chart 3: Retail Prices in the UK, 1900-1974
SOURCE: HMSO, see Appendix I.

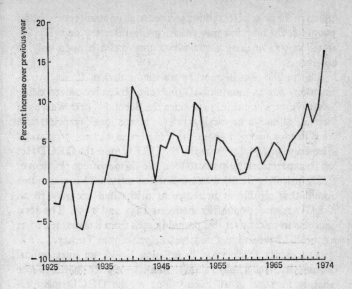

Chart 4: Annual increases in retail prices in the UK, 1950-74.
SOURCE: see Appendix I.

inflation the price of something seemed to go up almost every week; people could now imagine prices going up every day. Hyper-inflation was no longer something that could happen only to foreigners.

The public also became aware that inflation, if not hyper-inflation, was an international problem. Prices have been rising in all Western countries ever since the Second World War, as in Britain, although at varying rates. International agencies have long been concerned about the widespread nature of inflation. Sixteen years ago, for example, the OEEC (now the OECD) set up an expert working-party to look into the persistent problem of rising prices in its thirteen member countries. This committee found that significant increases in prices had occurred in all OECD member-countries between 1953 and 1959. The total increase in prices over this period ranged from a restrained 6 per cent in Switzerland to a massive 122 per cent in Turkey.

The recent acceleration in inflation is also an international phenomenon, as Table 6 shows. The rate of price-increases rose sharply in 1974 in all twenty-four of the OECD member-countries, to an average of 13 per cent. There was also an increase in every country (except, oddly, Turkey) in the previous year, when the average increase in prices rose from 5 to 8 per cent.

The causes of inflation

The world-wide nature of inflation must mean either that the same causes are operating everywhere or that inflation is a disease like smallpox that starts somewhere and quickly infects other parts of the world. To some extent, no doubt, economic relations between countries do transmit inflation from one to another. Increased import prices, especially of oil and other commodities such as sugar, are certainly one explanation, so that some can with justification blame the Arabs or the Ghanaians. Changes in the prices of these commodities, which account for a relatively small part of total expenditure, cannot, however, explain why almost all prices have risen so persistently. There are, moreover, plenty of other potential domestic causes operating seemingly independently in all countries to make international

	Annual rate			
	Average 1961–71	1972	1973	1974
Canada	2·9	4·8	7·6	10·7
United States	3·1	3·3	6·2	11·0
Japan	5·9	4·5	11·7	24·4
Australia	2·8	5·8	9·5	15·1
New Zealand	4·6	6·9	8·2	10·9
France	4·3	5·9	7·3	13·6
Germany	3·0	5·5	6·9	7·0
Italy	4·2	5·7	10·8	19·1
United Kingdom	4·6	7·1	9·2	16·0
Belgium	3·4	5·5	10·4	12·6
Luxembourg	3·0	5·2	6·1	9·5
Denmark	6·1	6·6	9·3	9·6
Ireland	5·4	8·7	11·4	15·2
Netherlands	4·8	7·8	8·0	17·0
Austria	3·7	6·3	7·6	9·5
Finland	5·4	7·4	11·4	17·4
Greece	2·2	4·4	15·5	26·9
Iceland	12·0	9·7	20·6	42·9
Norway	4·9	7·2	7·5	9·4
Portugal	5·5	10·7	12·9	25·1
Spain	6·8	8·3	11·4	15·6
Sweden	4·6	6·0	6·7	9·9
Switzerland	3·8	6·7	8·7	9·8
Turkey	7·4	15·5	14·0	23·8
OECD total	3·7	4·7	7·7	13·3
OECD Europe	4·2	6·5	8·7	12·8
EEC (enlarged)	4·0	6·2	8·3	12·6

SOURCE: *Economic Outlook* No. 16, OECD, December 1974, and *Main Economic Indicators*, OECD

Table 6: Annual Percentage Increases in Consumer Prices in OECD Member Countries, 1961–74

transmission of the disease untenable as a sole explanation.

In all countries, anyway, everyone deplores inflation and blames everyone else. The Arabs and the Ghanaians can with justification claim that they have in the past been exploited by the advanced countries which have paid for their primary products in currencies which have depreciated, so that the primary producers have had to pay more and more for their imports. Within the advanced countries, employers can blame trade unions' wage demands and the trade unions can, in times when profits have been rising or investment has been insufficient to keep down costs, blame the employers. Practically everyone blames governments to some extent, for excessive spending paid for by printing money, for allowing speculators to fuel the fires of inflation, or for other deficiencies according to the political beliefs of the critic.

Wherever the ultimate blame for inflation might lie, it is easy to see that inflation breeds upon itself. As prices rise, all the economic units in society – workers, consumers, and businessmen – try to restore their position. If costs increase, either through rising wages or increased material prices, then companies will want to increase their prices to restore profit margins. If consumer prices rise then workers will demand higher wages and, if they are unionized and confronting employers who can pass on the cost, may get them. If consumers or speculators expect prices to rise in the future as they have in the past, they will want to buy now rather than in the future, and their additional demand will help to push up prices now.

If all these factors are at work at a time when unemployment is low and factories are working to capacity, the increased demand for goods and services in the face of a slowly increasing supply will push up prices, but some of the factors will take effect even if there are unemployed resources.

The precise causes of inflation are a matter of dispute. Economists do not, of course, have any difficulty in identifying reasons for the inflation. What is difficult is to see where the process actually starts, and exactly how all these different economic units are *able* to raise their demands on output faster than output itself can increase. One explanation is simply that governments have been allowing the stock of money in the economy to rise faster than output; this is the so-called Monetarist view. Another is that the stock of money is not in itself important, and that prices rise either because strong labour bargaining-groups force up costs independently or because consumers, businessmen and the government decide to spend or invest more than the economic system can produce; this is the so-called Keynesian view.

It is the thesis of this book that in the past hundred years or so a series of interlinked and fundamental changes in the economy and in society have taken place which lie at the root of inflation. I shall also argue that the debate between the Monetarists and the Keynesians itself reflects different attitudes to these changes rather than purely technical matters about the way the economic system works and how it should be managed. To try to make this clear I shall have to sketch the changes that have taken place, and also go more deeply into the issues of the debate among economists. These two matters are dealt with successively in the next two chapters. First, however, it is convenient to have a look at the mechanism of fluctuations in economic activity which used to be regarded as the prime weakness in the capitalist system and which, until recently at least, seemed to have been cured at the expense of inflation.

Booms and slumps

Chart 5 shows the growth of real Gross Domestic Product (GDP)[1] in the UK between 1920 and 1973. (By 'real', I mean without the growth in the money value of GDP given by inflation.) In this period, GDP has actually declined by more than one per cent in only three years, all of them in the inter-war period. The sharpest decline was in 1921 when GDP fell by 13 per cent compared with the previous year, but there were also sharp falls of 4 per cent in 1926 and 6 per cent in 1931. The UK economy did not keep above its 1914 levels of output until after

1. The GDP is a measure of the (annual, in this instance) total flow of goods and services in the economy, *excluding* intermediate products (such as materials and components, thus avoiding double counting), the replacement of capital goods used up in the process of production, and net income from property and investment abroad. See GNP, page 107n.

1933 – this was twenty years of virtual stagnation. In the period since the Second World War, by contrast, output actually declined significantly in only two years, 1952 and 1955, and on both occasions real GDP fell by less than 1 per cent. In only one other year in the post-war period (1958) did real output fail to rise.

Like inflation, fluctuations in economic activity are not new, and upward and downward swings can be traced right back to the eighteenth century at least. Real GDP actually gives a damped view of these fluctuations, since even a 1 per cent decline in GDP can have major repercussions on employment. It can be seen from Chart 5 that unemployment has been much more volatile than real GDP, particularly in the inter-war period. But the striking feature of the chart is that, since the Second World War, unemployment has remained at very low levels and economic growth has been remarkably steady and rapid compared with the inter-war period.

How do fluctuations in business activity happen? Superficially at least, this is not a difficult question to answer because, as with inflation, the basic mechanism is fairly simple, although again the precise roles of all the factors that are thought to come into play are far from fully understood. Fluctuations occur because the processes of growth or decline in an economy tend to be both cumulative and self-limiting, so that any increase or decline in economic activity from whatever initial cause feeds upon itself. There are two ways in which increased activity in one industry affects others. The first is that at the bottom of the cycle an increase in activity in, say, the shoe industry will mean that shoemakers will take on additional workers. These workers will thus have more money to spend than when they were unemployed; this expenditure will generate increased activity in other industries, which may also take on additional labour, and this will in turn lead to further increases in demand, and so on. The second effect is that as shoe-production rises the manufacturers will order additional equipment; these orders will lead to additional activity in the capital goods industries whose workers' expenditure will also promote further demand elsewhere, and so on again. Now it so happens that increased demand in consumer-goods industries such as shoe-making tends to have a more than proportional effect upon the capital-goods industries like those

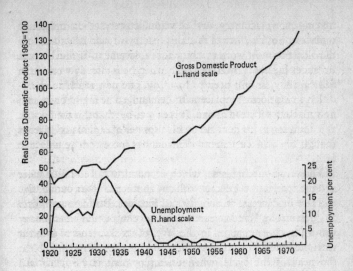

Chart 5: UK Gross Domestic Product at 1963 Prices and Unemployment 1920-73.

SOURCE: see Appendix I.

making shoe machinery. A shoe manufacturer, for example, may replace one of his stock of machines each year, and he will choose the oldest or most worn machine for replacement. If the demand for shoes increases by 20 per cent, when he is already working to full capacity, he will need to buy, say, one new machine in addition to his normal replacement demand, so he might order two new machines instead of one. It is easy to see that this would lead to a doubling in his demand on his supplier of capital goods, even though his own customers' demand has increased by only one fifth.

These two mechanisms, which economists call the multiplier and the accelerator, interact with one another to give a cumulative increase or decrease in activity and incomes. Business optimism or pessimism, credit expansion or contraction and many factors, such as changes in the level of stocks, tend to interact with the others in whichever direction the cycle is moving. Near the peak of the cycle, when unemployment is very low and capital equipment fully utilized, the growth of output inevitably slows down, since neither the consumer nor the capital-goods industries can expand by taking up idle capacity. Once consumption stops increasing, the increase in the demand for capital goods will also cease, and at this point the accelerator and multiplier work in a downward direction. The decline in activity reinforces itself as business confidence diminishes; even in those industries where demand is still increasing businessmen no longer expect this to continue and react by ceasing to invest.

A third mechanism, that of the price system, also operates with the business cycle, as I have already mentioned. In the upward movement, as demand increases faster than supply and shortages develop, prices rise; these higher prices improve profitability and provide businessmen with both the means and the incentive to invest, pressure is put on wages as labour becomes scarce, and increased spending further increases demand. In the downward part of the cycle, prices decline with demand, wage increases slow down, and interest rates fall as the demand for investment capital declines. It is this price mechanism which, in theory at least, helps the cycle to get out of its trough. Declining interest rates and prices should stimulate both investment and demand and set the cycle on an upward path again. This at least seemed to be the pattern in most cycles, especially in particular industries in the period up to the 1920s.

There is a vast literature on business-cycle theory and different writers have placed varying emphasis on the factors referred to in this oversimplified explanation. Some have introduced what might be called external factors that set the mechanism off, such as technical innovation or even sunspots; others have emphasized particular parts of the mechanism such as credit expansion and contraction; others still have identified further internal mechanisms such as the wearing out of capital equipment. A great deal of purely statistical analysis has been carried out to identify regular patterns of cyclical activity. Some of the patterns established are very complex, with minor oscillations moving around several longer cyclical trends, each of different length and amplitude, and all of them moving upwards as real output rises in the long term.

Another glance at Chart 5, particularly at the unemployment curve, will confirm the cyclical nature of the growth of real domestic product, although the cycles do not appear to be regular, and the different patterns of growth before and after the Second World War have already been noted. Since the war, cycles have been mainly restricted to fluctuations in the rate of growth of output (and prices, see Chart 4), while before the war the fluctuations in output were greater and included quite pronounced downward movements in output and prices (although these price movements did not always seem to follow the cycle as theory would suggest). I have yet to deal, however, with the stagnation and heavy unemployment that occurred in the 1920s and 1930s. This experience seems to be in conflict with the explanation I have given of the self-correcting nature of the business cycle.

In the 1920s and 1930s the cycle did not correct itself. As I have shown, it lasted in all for virtually two decades. The implication of economic understanding at the time was that all governments had to do was to work with economic forces, that is, to encourage interest rates and wages to decline. In fact, in a limited way this is what happened. The severe recession in 1921 was accompanied by a sharp fall in prices and wages. Between 1920 and 1922 prices and money wages fell by about one third. The government at the time had another reason for wanting a decline in the domestic price level. In 1919 Britain had left the gold standard, under which the value of the pound was fixed in terms of gold and could be exchanged for gold. This departure had been made necessary by the disruption caused by the First World War, but it was intended to return to gold as soon as possible. It was considered that a return to the gold standard was essential if the role of sterling as an international currency was to be preserved, as well as to maintain the value of the pound at home. Prices had risen sharply and Britain had lost its competitiveness in its export markets, which had also been neglected during the war. The government wished to return to the pre-war parity of $4.87. It did this in 1925 but, despite the fall in prices that had occurred since the war, British exports were still not fully competitive and it was clear that if the parity was to be maintained further falls in prices were necessary. The government's attempts to get wages down culminated in the General Strike of 1926. Prices did in fact continue to fall throughout the 1920s and 1930s but wage rates remained at around the levels of 1926, so that real wages – for those in employment – rose over the period.

The war had left the economies of all the European belligerents in disarray but, other than in Britain (and in Germany, where 1921–2 saw the famous 'suitcases of money' hyper-inflation), the 1920s was not a period of general massive unemployment and dislocation on a world scale. Indeed in the United States, after a short post-war recession in 1921 in which real GDP did not fall, although unemployment rose to 11 per cent, the rest of the 1920s was a period of boom which only ended in 1928, being followed in 1929 by the Stock Market Crash. From 1930 onwards, however, the slump spread as US imports declined and its investment abroad fell off. Britain's overseas position was too weak to maintain its fixed exchange rate in the face of the massive fall in world trade and the disruption of the international credit system which ensued, and it was forced off the gold standard in 1931. Unemployment in the United States rose to a quarter of the labour force in 1933, and both there and in Germany the economic situation became much worse than in Britain.

As the years of depression dragged on in Britain, the apparent lack of responsiveness of the economy to declining prices was the subject of great debate among economists. If prices and wages fell far enough, argued some economists, investment would be resumed and growth restored on a sound basis. Many believed that the new strength of trade unionism and the spread of monopolistic conditions in many industries were delaying this natural process of adjustment and were actually responsible for the failure of the economy to recover from the slump as it always had in previous cycles. From the early 1920s John Maynard Keynes had argued against a return to the gold standard at the pre-war parity and against attempts to push down wages. He thought that the government should impose protective measures to reduce imports and embark upon a major programme of investment in public works, something which Lloyd George and others were also advocating. Keynes argued that the government should not be trying to balance its budget by cutting expenditure and increasing taxation; on the contrary, it should be running a deficit to help stimulate demand. The Treasury was, however, strongly opposed to deficit financing and believed that savings were limited, so that if the government borrowed money to pay for public investment there would be less available in the capital market to finance private investment. Public investment would thus be substituted for private investment without increasing the total.

Keynes's advice was not, therefore, taken to any significant extent and the views of the economic establishment – the classical economists, as he called them – prevailed. Some people think that this was at least partly because Keynes's views were not based on, or at least not expressed in terms of, a comprehensive and internally consistent theory of the workings of the economy. Keynes did rectify this by the publication in 1936 of his *General Theory of Employment, Interest and Money*. The General Theory attempted to explain how it was quite possible for an economy to be in equilibrium at far below full employment and to remain there indefinitely whatever happened to wages and prices. This book was to have enormous influence later, but it came too late to affect events significantly at the time. The governments of the late 1930s continued to pursue balanced budgets, and although unemployment declined from 1933 onwards it was not to fall below 10 per cent until 1940.

In restrospect it now appears that Keynes was right and that many other economists at the time were wrong. Although we cannot even now be sure of the extent to which his technical analysis of the causes of unemployment in the inter-war period was correct, there seems little doubt that a massive programme of government spending of the kind he proposed would have accelerated recovery. There is more doubt, however, about the extent to which his insights into the workings of the inter-war economy can help us in the very different situation of the 1970s.

Stag-flation

The pursuit of Keynesian policies since the war has certainly been accompanied by low unemployment and rapid economic growth. Indeed, the only interruptions to that growth in Britain have been caused by deliberate government action to reduce inflationary pressures in the interests of the balance of payments. For Keynesian economics does not consist only in the discovery that it is possible to spend your way out of a recession; its analysis leads also to the prescription of a budget surplus (among other measures) when demand is excessive and resources are fully employed.

These 'dabs on the brake' (Chancellors of the Exchequer have frequently been fond of motoring analogies) have, however, had to be followed by bursts of acceleration, as a slowing down in economic growth (and price increases) has soon resulted in a sharp increase in unemployment. This has happened not so much because the Chancellors' brakes have worked too quickly than because they have often been applied too late, that is, at a time when demand was beginning to fall off of its own accord. In the same way, bursts on the accelerator have also come at a time when the pressure of demand was beginning to increase again. Thus, Keynesian policies have not eliminated the business cycle (investment in particular has continued to fluctuate), nor have they eliminated the need for structural change in the economy as technology and changing tastes require a decline in some industries and growth in others.

After some twenty years of the pursuit of Keynesian policies, inflation has grown to the point where it creates a dilemma for governments.

The dilemma is that the need to maintain employment requires the stimulation of demand, while the need to slow down the rate of increase in prices apparently requires the opposite course of action. Governments reacted to the sharp increase in inflation in 1973–4 by measures to slow down demand, but at the time of writing (March 1975) the United States at least is now stimulating demand to prevent a further rise in unemployment. Meanwhile, in that and most other advanced countries output is stagnant and prices continue to rise. Stag-flation is a new situation, in the face of which Keynesian policies appear impotent.

7. The Centripetal Society

The inflation machine

Much has been written about the rise of the state, the concentration of business and the growth of trade unionism in Western societies, but only a few writers have drawn attention to the inter-relationships between these things and their common source in the rise of affluent democracy. For the last hundred years or more, powerful centripetal[1] forces have been at work to centralize the institutions controlling economic activity in these countries. It is the object of this chapter, the longest and perhaps the most important in the book, to sketch these forces and to show how they have contributed to inflation.

The process can be summarized quite briefly. Rising wealth has liberated consumers from preoccupation with day-to-day survival and resulted in more demands for security, and the expectation of, and demand for, continuing improvements in living standards. Democratic pressure on government has led to continually increasing efforts by the state to respond to these demands, both directly and by more and more intervention in economic affairs. The increased role of the state has required higher taxation and this, together with increased intervention, has led to the gradual transformation of the private sector from a competitive atomistic system, responding to consumer wishes through the price mechanism, to a system of very large units controlling, rather than being controlled by, their markets and heavily dependent upon increasing state intervention. The concentration of business has both stimulated the development of the trade-union movement and been furthered by it. Trade unions have increased the pressure on governments to maintain high levels of employment and have also increased the incomes of their members at the expense

1. 'Centripetal' means 'tending towards the centre', and it is the antonym of 'centrifugal'.

of unorganized workers and the self-employed, thus encouraging these in turn to become organized. Attempts by each sector of society – employees, the state, business – to increase its own share of output at the expense of the others and increasing rigidities in the system which have delayed adjustment to changes made necessary by evolving technology and tastes have created tensions which have been partially resolved by rising prices. The price increases required to release these tensions have, however, tended to grow as members of society have become accustomed to inflation and as the system has become more centralized and the scope for the growth of centralized institutions at the expense of the decentralized has diminished.

I have depicted these institutional elements in society and some of their interactions in Chart 6. Consumers, the state, business and the trades unions are represented as four segments of a wheel revolving round an axle of increasing wealth. The spokes of the wheel symbolize the inter-connections between the various elements. Those who like comprehensiveness and have a mechanical turn of mind may imagine the hub of the wheel as containing a friction clutch which represents the monetary system. If the wheel is revolving round a helix so that it rises or falls as output or wealth rises or falls, then the speed with which the wheel spins for any given movement up or down the helix can be thought of as being proportionate to the rate of change of prices. The hub of the wheel, the monetary system, would in this way accommodate changes in the money value of output to changes in real output, so that when prices were rising rapidly the wheel could spin very rapidly while moving up the helix only very slowly.

It doesn't matter where we start in having a more detailed look at the inflation wheel, because a circle has no beginning, but there is real logic, and political neutrality, in beginning with the consumer. I should make it clear that what follows is only the briefest outline of the process. For example, I have dealt only with the power base of the main elements in society, not with the particular institutions, such as political parties, government departments, the shop floor, the TUC, companies and the CBI, that actually exert that power or are involved in channelling it.

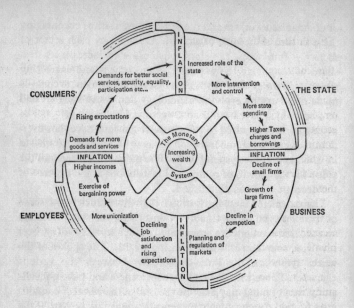

Chart 6: The Inflation Machine.

The role of the consumer

The consumer is, of course, everyone in society, since we all consume. Many of us also play another of the roles marked on the wheel, as an employee in the public or private sector, or as an employer or a self-employed person in business. The recent economic history of Western economies has been very much dominated by the development of the consumer society, a society in which more and more goods and services have been bought by consumers in an increasingly sophisticated marketing environment.

The range of consumer durables which the average home might possess has been extended since the war from a radio, a vacuum cleaner, a cooker and perhaps a boiler, to a refrigerator, a telephone, a washing machine, a TV set, and many other things such as electric razors, cars, hi-fi and space heating.

Diet, too, has become more varied, with vastly increased consumption of prepared foods, more alcohol and more meat. Standards of clothing are much higher, especially for lower-income households. The life of the average consumer has been enriched by many other things – better housing, occasional holidays abroad, and so on. At the same time, methods of marketing and consumer credit have developed: the emergence of the supermarket, universally available credit and the persuasiveness of advertising have combined to make it easier and more agreeable to consume, and to keep consumption at high and increasing levels.

This extension of the American pattern for consumption to other countries, which is what has been happening, has reflected enormously increased real incomes and output. The United States is still a long way ahead of most other countries. US Gross National Product (GNP)[1] in 1970 was of the order of $995 billion; that is, America produces $4,800 each year for every man, woman and child in the country.

In Sweden the corresponding figure was $3,840, in France it

1. The GNP is equal to the sum of all income (including rent and profits) in the economy, (GDP), but before allowing for the using up of the nation's capital stock *plus* net income from abroad. When capital consumption is subtracted it is called the national income.

was $2,900, and in the UK $2,200. In fact, comparisons of this kind between countries are far from accurate. This is because the figures are arrived at by converting GNP figures in local currency at current international exchange rates with the dollar, and exchange rates do not necessarily reflect internal purchasing power. What is important is that these levels of output are vastly higher than they were 100 years ago. It can be seen from Table 7 that in the United Kingdom, where growth has been slowest among the four countries shown, GNP was two and a half times the 1870 level a century later.

	Per cent
United States	186
France	190
Sweden	241
UK	147

SOURCE: A. Maddison, *Economic Growth in the West*, Allen & Unwin, 1964; extended to 1970 from OECD sources.

Table 7: Increase in Real GNP Per Head in Selected Countries, 1870–1970

The increases in Table 7 are in real terms; that is to say, they allow for the decline in the value of money which has taken place over this period. In money terms, of course, increases in output per head have been very much faster; although consumer prices fell over the period 1870–1900, they have risen ten times since 1900.

For statistical convenience I have shown these changes in terms of output per head, but increases in earnings have been even more striking. In the UK, an adult worker in manufacturing earning £1·40 a week in 1900 would have been earning about £41 a week in 1973 at current prices. This would be something like £4·50 at the prices obtaining in 1900. These increases in pre-tax wages reflect both the increase in total output that occurred over the period, and also some redistribution of the national income in favour of wage-earners and the retired, and away from profits, rents and the self-employed, trends which are still going on today and to which I shall return later.

Although it is one thing to put down statistical comparisons of this sort and quite another to be sure what they mean in tangible terms, there is no doubt that a massive increase in incomes and consumption has occurred in Britain and other advanced countries in the last hundred years. Moreover, except in wartime, this increase in incomes has occurred almost continuously throughout the period, even – for those in employment – during the 1930s. The increase also goes back a long way in time: for example, real incomes per head in Britain rose by about one third between 1855 and 1870; so real incomes have been rising now, with only minor interruptions, for the last 130 years and longer.

This increase in the personal income and wealth of the mass of the population over a very long period is bringing about fundamental changes in the whole nature of society and the economic system. Some of these changes we can see and trace back to the increased wealth that has stimulated them; others we can only guess at. Joe Roeber, in his book, *The Organisation in a Changing Environment*, compares the effects of increased wealth on society with those of a rising tide on the landscape:

If the ice-cap of Greenland was melted, I remember being told at school, the level of the seas around the world would rise by perhaps six inches. And the result would be the loss of huge tracts of land along the coastal strips of all the countries of the world. An inch or so more and yet more land would disappear: valleys would become inlets, plains become oceans, hills become islands. I always found it an oddly frightening thought; the effect seems so disproportionate to the cause. It is no less frightening and disproportionate than the effects on society of quite modest increases in wealth. The tide of wealth is creeping up by fractions of an inch, and each advance is obliterating whole continents of inherited attitudes and accepted relationships. Our social landscape is being transformed. And this is being achieved by granting to the majority of people in the prosperous West two things, the secure expectation of the satisfaction of basic material needs and the privilege of choice, which revoke from the social systems the power to coerce their members.

The more materially secure man has become – as the rising

tide of wealth has brought freedom from want of basic necessities to the bulk of the population on a scale undreamed of 150 years ago – the more security he has demanded. The result has been pressure on the state by the electorate to provide social security on an increasing scale including health and education, housing, security of employment, retirement benefits and other public services. Greater security has liberated man from dependence upon others and has thus enhanced his freedom to demand more freedom.

Increased wealth and the changes it has made possible have not made mankind content, however much his lot has improved. The more goods and services consumers have had the more they want; the more equal men have become the more concerned they are with remaining inequalities, not merely material inequalities, but inequalities of education, social mobility and opportunity.

The long, continuing improvement in material welfare has led to firmly based expectations that this improvement will continue, and its more recent association with continuing rising prices has led to the expectation that prices too will continue to increase. Pressure on available resources has mounted, therefore, and resistance to price-increases has progressively diminished; both these things have helped to keep prices rising.

Part of the effect of consumers' expectations of continuing price-rises in reinforcing inflation is that these rises encourage borrowing to finance expenditure. Indeed, an important element in the 'Americanization' of consumption has been the transfer to Europe of increasingly sophisticated methods of consumer credit which have encouraged consumer indebtedness to increase steadily. (The most recent of these devices is the credit card.) Although the consumer is frequently accused of being unsophisticated about the desirability of incurring debt in inflationary periods, this lack of sophistication has not prevented him from rapidly increasing his borrowing. Many consumers have found that as their incomes rise the burden of fixed repayments falls, and this encourages them to borrow more. House-owners have until recently become accustomed to an apparently inexorable appreciation in the value of their properties.

It will take the rest of this book to bring out the fuller implications of increased wealth and expectations, but it was important to start where the problem of inflation starts, firmly in the hands of the consumer and the electorate.

The role of the state

The demand of consumers for more social services and job security has led to a great increase in the role of the state in the economy.[1] This role has also increased to meet the rising costs of defence and the exercise of power politics, as weapons have become more complex. There has also been an increase in the role of the state in peaceful technological development, in the belief that some kinds of technology require public intervention. Whether this belief is justified does not concern me here; but it is an additional factor in expanding the role of the state.

Like increased wealth, the share of the state in the national product has been edging up over a very long period. Table 8 shows that the share of income from employment in the public sector (including central and local government but excluding public corporations) was only 3 per cent of the GDP in 1907. By the 1920s and 1930s it had risen to nearly 5 per cent. A very large further increase occurred in the Second World War and the share of employees of central and local government in GDP is still increasing. In 1973 it reached almost 13 per cent – more than four times the level at the beginning of the twentieth century.

The state also owns and operates much of industry in Britain. If this is allowed for, the public sector employs well over a quarter of the working population and accounted in 1973 for 27 per cent of GDP. Since the facts are easily available but so little-known, it is worth looking at changes in public-sector employment in some detail. The total number of persons in employment in the UK has changed little in the last decade, despite increasing total population (there has been an increase in unemployment and a considerable advance in the age of retirement). Yet employment in the public sector rose by nearly one million between 1961 and 1973, mainly in local government, at the expense of an *absolute decline in employment in the private sector* of just over 1 million. In

1. Except where specifically excluded, I use the term 'state' to include central and local government and the nationalized industries.

1907	3·0
1924	4·8
1935	4·8
1949	9·2
1955	9·3
1964	10·1
1973	12·9

(Income from employment includes public administration and defence, the public health service and local authority educational services. The 1907 figure refers to Great Britain.)

SOURCE: P. Deane and W. A. Cole, *British Economic Growth 1688–1959*, Cambridge University Press; and *National Income and Expenditure*, 1973, HMSO

Table 8: Income from Employment in the UK Public Sector as Percentage of the GDP

this period, therefore, a million people – 5 per cent of all private sector employees – shifted into the public sector. The numbers employed in the private sector and different parts of the public sector are given in Table 9.

Within the public sector there were some interesting changes in the pattern of employment. Industrial employment by the public sector actually fell sharply over the last decade, mainly

	Total in employ-ment	Total public sector	Central govern-ment	Local authori-ties	Public corpora-tions	Private sector
1961	22,824	5,280	1,302	1,782	2,196	17,544
1973	22,662	6,180	1,608	2,714	1,858	16,482

(HM Forces are excluded. The basis of the statistics changed in 1971, but this does not affect the broad conclusions drawn in the text.)

SOURCE: *Economic Trends*, HMSO

Table 9: Employment in the Public and Private Sectors of the UK Economy, 1961 and 1973

through the shedding of labour by the coal industry and nationalized transport undertakings, although this trend will be reversed in the future if the government's plans to nationalize the aerospace, ports and other industries are put into effect. Two thirds of the increase in central government employment was accounted for by the Health Service, but numbers in all departments of government except defence increased rapidly. By far the largest increase in employment occurred among local authorities, the bulk of it concentrated in education, health and welfare.

It can be argued that even the figures given so far greatly understate the role of the state in the economy, particularly from the point of view of cash flows. For, in addition to its own direct expenditure, the state takes money away from some parts of the community and gives it back to others by means of subsidies and cash grants to persons and institutions. The state also pays interest on its debts. If all these expenditures are taken account of we find that total state expenditure, on capital and current account, was 51 per cent of the value of the GNP in 1973.

To meet increasing national expenditure the state has had to increase its income and indeed, over the long period, its share of the national income by increasing taxes and by other means. It is common knowledge that income taxes are now enormously higher than they were before the First World War (although they are lower than during the Second World War). In 1900 the standard rate of income tax was 5 per cent, in 1925 it was 20 per cent, and now the basic rate is 33 per cent. The intricacies of the tax system mean that these figures are not really comparable, but they give a rough impression of the pace of increase. Income tax is, of course, far from being the only source of tax revenue: there are also value-added tax (VAT), customs and excise duties, capital gains taxes, capital transfer taxes and corporation tax.

In 1973 the state collected personal and company taxes, rates and national insurance contributions amounting to over £8 a week for every man, woman and child in the country. Even after company grants, pensions and other transfer payments are allowed for, the net amount was still about £5 per head per week – about 80 per cent more in real terms than in 1950. It will surprise most people to learn that state revenue defined in this way was the same proportion of the national income – 42 per cent before transfer payments and about 26 per cent after these payments – in both 1950 and 1973, although it did fall in the 1960s and has risen since.

The state is not, however, as parsimonious as these surprising statistics suggest, for it pretty consistently spends more than it receives from taxes, rates, social-security contributions and net income from its trading activities. The difference is called the borrowing requirement, which, in the eleven years 1963–73, was a negative amount in 1969 and 1970 (when the government was paying off debt), was positive in all other years, and rose from 7·5 per cent of total state expenditure in 1972 to 13 per cent in 1973.

The state borrowing requirement was £4,222 million in 1973, and of this central government accounted for just under half, or £2,034 million. Of the remainder the local authorities accounted for about three fifths and the public corporations two fifths, although in practice these two parts of the public sector also borrow from the government, so that some of central government's borrowing is made on their behalf rather than on its own. The extent to which state spending from borrowed money is inflationary depends upon two things. First, as I explained in Chapter 6, state spending will probably not be inflationary, at least not to any significant extent, where there is slack capacity throughout the economy; in these conditions, like any other spending, it will raise employment rather than prices. Second, even where employment is fairly full, as it has been during most of the post-war period, state spending will not add to the general pressure of demand where it is simply the result of substituting public expenditure for private expenditure. This in turn will depend mainly on how the borrowing is financed.

In fact, the greater part of government borrowing is financed in ways which do not neutralize expenditure that might otherwise have been made by the public, and which results moreover in increasing the stock of money. In 1973, half of the borrowing requirement of the central government was financed simply by borrowing from the Bank of England and a quarter was financed by increasing the amount of notes and coin in circulation, usually referred to as 'printing money'. Both these methods increase the stock of money but do nothing to neutralize expenditure by the public. The other principal means of financing the borrowing requirement, sales of government securities, will affect the money supply and public spending differently according to whether or not these securities are purchased by members of the public, banks or other institutions, and according to other factors which it would unnecessarily complicate my account to explain here. Overseas borrowing or lending by the government also complicates the picture, but it is true to say that the means used by government to finance its borrowing requirement have in most recent years been overwhelmingly inflationary under the conditions of full employment which generally prevailed, both in the sense that they have led to an increase in the supply of money and because they have not led to a substitution of government spending for private spending, but have increased total expenditure. The reader will learn in the next chapter that although there is some dispute about whether or not increasing the money supply is ever inflationary it is generally agreed among economists that an increase in total spending under conditions of full employment will always push up prices. Thus there can be little doubt that the manner in which public finance has been managed in recent years has contributed to inflationary pressures.

In summary, therefore, in this century as a whole the government has been financing an increasing share of national expenditure, first by increasing its share of national income through higher taxes and other current revenues. But, particularly since the Second World War, it has also and less obviously been increasing its share of national expenditure faster than its share of national income by borrowing in a way that has increased inflationary pressures. This has meant that the burden of servicing the national debt – what the state owes to the public and to governments and the public abroad – has steadily risen. This burden has been rising much faster in money terms than in real terms: between 1963 and 1973, for example, the cost of servicing the national debt rose by 126 per cent, but the real burden, after allowing for the decline in the value of money that occurred over the period, rose by only about one third. So while public expenditure has contributed to inflation, inflation has enabled the state to increase its share of total expenditure faster than its share of income, and less painfully than would otherwise have been the case. Public finance also benefits from inflation in another way known as 'fiscal drag'. As incomes rise in money terms, the yields of taxes which rise progressively with income also increase without any change in the tax rates. The same thing happens with what are called *ad valorem* taxes such as VAT.

The role of the state in the inflationary process is not limited to its domestic activities. The government also spends money abroad, on defence, foreign representation and aid, offsetting some of the overseas earnings of the private sector. (The government has some earnings abroad, but they are very small in relation to its expenditure.) Thus, the government increases the demand for imports while doing little to increase exports. The state also borrows abroad and this too may be inflationary unless steps are taken to neutralize the effect of inflows of money from abroad upon the stock of money and spending by the public.

The state, in its search for greater freedom to determine its desired expenditure (and employment levels) at home, seems now to have permanently abandoned fixed exchange rates. Under the gold standard, which operated before the First World War, and also effectively under the gold-exchange standard to which Britain returned in the 1920s, exchange rates were fixed and gold movements were used to settle balance-of-payments surpluses and deficits. Since the domestic currency was tied to gold, countries which were losing gold, through spending more abroad than they earned (had balance of payments deficits) were obliged to restrict the money supply and government expenditure. This damped economic activity and had the effect of reducing the demand for imports and creating more room for exports. The reverse occurred when gold flowed into a country as a result of a balance-of-payments surplus. The reason Britain left the gold standard in 1931 was that loss of gold had led to an unacceptably severe contraction of output and employment in the circumstances of the world depression.

Today, after a long period of semi-fixed exchange rates maintained in part through cooperation in the International Monetary Fund (IMF), we have a system of floating exchange rates among many of the principal trading countries. Under this system exchange rates are not fixed, but vary with the supply and demand for the country's currency. When a country runs a balance-of-payments deficit (either because it is importing more goods and services than it is exporting or because capital is moving out of the country) its currency becomes weaker and its price in terms of other currencies drops. Unfortunately, as I explained in Chapter 1, this means that the cost of imports rises, putting pressure on domestic prices, especially in a country like Britain which imports a great deal of its food and raw materials. Thus, under the gold standard a payments deficit led to a fall in domestic activity and prices while the cost of imports remained unchanged, whereas under floating exchange rates imports become more expensive. Unless a downward float is accompanied by measures to reduce domestic activity, it tends to be inflationary. For this reason exchange rates are in fact 'managed' to some extent. A country's central bank can enter the currency market, using its reserves of gold and foreign exchange to buy its own currency and thus helping to keep its price up.

The role of business

The organization of business in the private sector has also altered radically in the past hundred years, and in ways which contribute to the inflationary process to a considerable extent. These changes manifest themselves principally in the enormously increased size of business units in all Western countries and in a transformation in the nature of their ownership and control.

In the middle of the nineteenth century, with the exception of a small number of state-approved monopolies, all businesses were very small by today's standards and were for the most part managed by their owners. They were, in short, like the small businesses of today, familiar in farming or in the service trades, and exemplified by independent garages and the smaller retail shops. In these firms the owner has inherited the business or has saved or borrowed the necessary capital and started it himself. With his family and perhaps one or more partners, he also directs it, in competition with many thousands of other firms of similar size.

There are, of course, many small businesses left in Britain, over a million and a quarter of them, but they account for a diminishing proportion of total output. Small business is giving way to the giant corporation whose activities extend over many products and many countries and which is as different from small business as a jumbo-jet from a beetle. Although there are about 275,000 incorporated businesses in Britain (the rest are sole traders and partnerships), a mere 4,000 or so account for 75 per cent of corporate profits. A mere 100 or so account for approaching half of total profits in manufacturing. These are the great oil, motor, chemical and food and drink companies that are household names, such as Imperial Tobacco, Unilever, Ford and ICI.

Table 10 shows how the share of the 100 largest companies in manufacturing net output[1] has increased this century.

	Share %		Share %
1909	16	1958	33
1924	21	1963	38
1935	24	1968	42
1949	31	1970	45
1953	26		

SOURCE: S. J. Prais, 'A New Look at the Growth of Industrial Concentration', Oxford Economic Papers, July 1974

Table 10: Share of the Hundred Largest Manufacturing Enterprises in New Output in Britain, 1909–70

It can be seen that, except immediately after the Second World War, the share of the giant companies was higher in every census year throughout the period, and that since that time the rate of increase has accelerated.

The emergence of the giant company dates back to the early nineteenth century and the introduction of limited liability. This meant that people wishing to invest in business could do so without committing their whole material fortune to the success of

1. Net output is the difference between the sales revenue of a firm and the value of the materials and components obtained outside the firm and used in the production process. It is an approximate indication of the size of the contribution of a firm to the GNP.

the enterprise. A sole trader or a partner in a business without limited liability is responsible for the debts of the business to the extent of his entire wealth: he does not mind this because he controls directly the growth of the liabilities of his firm. The shareholder in a limited company is responsible for its debts only to the extent of his shareholding: that is normally the most he can lose.

The development of the factory system and technological change in production and transportation greatly increased the capital requirements of business and the opportunities for growth in the nineteenth century. At first, companies such as the great British railway companies were created by Act of Parliament, but this became too cumbersome and from 1825 it became possible to form limited joint stock companies by registration; later still this was extended to private companies. The result was a tremendous growth in corporate business. As time went by some large companies grew and prospered, others fell by the wayside and the average size of companies increased. The more successful acquired their competitors and in some markets gradually achieved a position of great strength where they could not be challenged by newcomers. This process has continued so that today a small number of large firms control the bulk of sales in most major industries in Britain.

At first, joint stock companies were directed by persons who had major, often controlling, shareholdings. As the companies grew in size and issued more equity capital these shareholdings were diluted. Gradually ownership and control of companies became separated, until today the typical board of directors that control and run the business are remunerated mainly by salary and own only a few per cent, at most, of the stock of their company. The shareholders are, increasingly, other larger companies – financial institutions such as insurance companies, unit trusts and pension funds – which hold the wealth of the ordinary citizen, who thus owns big business (at one or two removes) but has little control over it.

As the state itself has grown it has, as I have shown, had to increase taxation; this has played an important part in accelerating the changes I have been describing. Death duties have forced private companies to seek stock-exchange quotations so that parts of the business can be sold off to the general public to meet these taxes. More important, the taxation of personal income and wealth has meant that the individual owner of a small business has found it more and more difficult to finance the growth of his enterprise from his own resources. True, the capital market has greatly increased in size and complexity in the past century, but there are many obstacles to the use of institutional finance by small business. The most important one may be the motivation of the small businessman himself. He is a businessman on his own account because he wishes to be independent, and he will be reluctant to go to outside sources of finance where this means loss of control. It is also difficult and costly for any large institution to assess the prospects of the thousands of firms each year which need relatively small amounts of cash to develop.

These difficulties do not arise with the giant company: it requires funds in large amounts which justify thorough investigation; moreover, investment in a large company involves less risk, a factor which makes it more attractive to the large investor. Finally, and most important, the directors of a large company are not the owners of the business they control and are less concerned with the effect of borrowing upon their independence. As a result of all these factors capital markets are now increasingly channelling investment funds towards the large company and away from the small firm.

The state has helped to accelerate the growth of the giant corporation and the decline of the small in many other ways, by both commission and omission. Although governments of all political complexions have proclaimed the virtues of competition in the private sector, they have done little to preserve it. The only way to preserve competition would have been to arrest the growth of the giant companies, and this would not be easy to do. Nor in most senses is it in the interest of the state to do this. It is much easier for the state, as it becomes more and more involved in the economy, to deal with a few large companies than with large numbers of small ones. The officials of the state also have much more in common with the officials of large companies, since both share a representative role in the context of a large organization, than with the owners of small businesses who represent only themselves.

Most people readily understand how the role of the state has grown this century, and also how the increasing wealth of consumers has given them a basis for expecting further increases in material well-being within a framework of social security provided by the state. Many will accept the possibility that these two factors contribute to inflation. The role of business and its concentration is more difficult to understand: there seems to be a mental blockage in most people which prevents them from seeing how fundamental the changes I have been describing really are. It is for this reason and not necessarily because it is more important, that I have devoted as much space to the role of business in the inflationary process as to the role of the state itself.

One of the most important consequences of the separation of ownership from control in the large company has been a change in the motivation of the typical business leader. Since he has little or no personal shareholding he will be more concerned with the size and growth and security of the business that employs him (also with certain other benefits such as the exercise of power or technical virtuosity) than with maximizing profits. In general, the larger the company the higher the salaries of its officers and the stronger their security of tenure. Of course, profit remains important, for a number of reasons, but it is naturally a less vital concern when it does not go directly into the pocket of the person who is responsible for making it.

John Kenneth Galbraith has analysed this change in motivation resulting from the emergence of the giant company in his famous book *The New Industrial State*. He also explains how, in the markets dominated by these companies, the risks associated with their investment in plant and organization are such that the consumer cannot be allowed complete freedom to determine the quantities and prices of the goods the companies supply. The security and the growth of the organization would be placed in jeopardy if it were completely at the mercy of the consumer's whims. The threat from competition has been effectively blocked off by the reduction of the number of firms in the market place to two or three. These share a common interest in survival and are most reluctant to engage in the nuclear warfare of price competition which could destroy them all. These firms, therefore, do not compete in price or quality to any significant extent, but concentrate upon persuading the consumer to buy what they can most conveniently supply. They exert control over the consumer by controlling sales outlets wherever possible, and by advertising and other means of sales promotion. In many instances, of course, the most important customer of these companies is the state itself.

As far as possible the giant companies also attempt to secure themselves against shortfalls in the supply of finance or raw materials, or increases in costs that might prevent them from maintaining the growth of sales to the consumer. They do this by contracts with their suppliers, usually giant companies like themselves; in the end, however, they can, within broad limits, pass on higher costs or compensate for shortages of supply by increasing prices to the consumer.

The giant companies will not normally be restrained by competition from raising their prices because their competitors will be anxious to avoid price competition and will all, in any event, be suffering from the same pressures to raise prices. The consumer will normally have little choice but to accept the price increases; the pain will be eased as far as possible for him either by reductions in the quality or quantity of the goods supplied, while prices remain the same, or by increased prices accompanied by real or imaginary improvements to the product. To a major extent, the large corporations are heavily concentrated in markets where the products are regarded as essentials by consumers – drinks, petrol, bread – and where resistance to price increases is low. A consequence of the largest companies' great size (and hence exposed position) and interdependence with the state is, however, that they take a very broad view of their interests. Gross exploitation of the consumer is prevented by the fear that it would lead to a loss of the freedom from outside interference which they cherish. Thus, to an increasing extent, the role of competition and the price mechanism is being replaced by a more general pressure from the public interest.

Just as inflation brings some benefits to the state, so it benefits the large corporations through the reduction in the burden of debt repayment. Since the largest companies can borrow at the lowest rates they can use borrowed capital to acquire other smaller companies, thus speeding up their own growth.

In fact, in the United States and almost certainly in Britain too, most of the increase in the share of the largest companies in output has come about not because they have been able to expand sales at the expense of their competitors but because they have acquired their (smaller) competitors lock stock and barrel. The rest of the increase in their share can be explained by the fact that large companies tend to be concentrated in the fastest-growing industries. As the large companies have penetrated deeper and deeper into the competitive sector of the economy, scope for their growth has diminished and the inflationary effect of their attempts to secure continued growth has become more powerful.

The role of the trade unions

It was illegal to organize a trade union in Britain before 1824, and the development of trade unions paralleled the development of the factory system: as workpeople were gathered together in towns and factories, no longer in dispersed employment in their homes and in agriculture, so they began to organize themselves to bargain with their employers. The early days of the movement were a struggle, not only for better pay and conditions but also for political recognition. This was finally achieved with the Trades Union Act of 1871. Trade-union membership grew rapidly in the 1880s, and by 1890 Britain had the most organized labour force among all the advanced countries, with about 8 per cent of its industrial workers in unions.

Table 11 shows that an enormous increase in trade-union membership occurred between the opening of the twentieth century and 1920. This was stimulated by the decline in real wage-rates and, to a lesser extent, earnings that occurred during the 1914–18 war through inflation, and after the war when it became government policy to force real wages down to permit a return to the gold standard at the pre-war parity. Not surprisingly labour relations deteriorated after the war, with great increases in strikes. With the high unemployment of the 1920s and 1930s trade-union membership fell. As with the First, the Second World War was accompanied by an increase in trade-union membership, although 1920 membership levels were unsurpassed until 1950. Since then membership has fluctuated but has

	Number of trade unions at end year	Membership at end year, thousands	Percentage of labour force in trade unions
1892	1,233	1,559	10
1900	1,323	2,022	12
1910	1,269	2,565	14
1920	1,384	8,348	40
1930	1,121	4,842	23
1940	1,004	6,613	28
1950	732	9,289	42
1960	664	9,835	41
1965	608	10,318	41
1970	513	11,168	45
1972	466	11,315	46

SOURCE: *British Labour Statistics: Historical Abstract 1886–1968*, HMSO; *British Labour Statistics: 1972 Yearbook*, HMSO

Table 11: Numbers of Trade Unions in Britain, and Their Membership as a Percentage of the Total Labour Force, 1892–1972

increased overall, especially since the mid 1960s when increases in real wages slowed down.

Today the proportion of the working population in unions is rapidly approaching 50 per cent. Unionization is no longer mainly restricted to industrial and manual workers but is also progressively increasing among white-collar workers, who now account for about 40 per cent of the total. It is also increasing fast among women. In 1972 2·9 million women were members of trade unions and women accounted for 60 per cent of the growth in total union membership between 1950 and 1972. As the membership of trade unions has grown, the number of unions has declined. This has come about by amalgamation of existing unions and the extension of membership across traditional industry or craft borderlines. Like concentration among industrial companies, this process has quickened in the period since 1950. Over three quarters of trade-union members are in the 23 largest unions, and well over half are in the top 10.

Membership of trade unions is highest in the public sector – in coal-mining and railways it is 100 per cent. In the private sector it is highest in the industries dominated by large companies, such as the motor industry. It is lowest among small firms. A survey conducted by the Committee of Inquiry on Small Firms in 1969 found that only 8 per cent of small firms in manufacturing and 5 per cent in non-manufacturing industries were entirely unionized. The proportion of firms unionized rose sharply with the size of firm and also tended to be higher in the more slow-growing firms, reflecting the general tendency for unionization, in times of full employment at least, to increase most rapidly when the growth of real wages slows down.

Periods of increasing trade-union membership also appear to have been periods of increased strikes, although the 1920s were an exception to this: in terms of working-days lost even recent industrial disputes have been much less severe than those in the late 1910s and 1920s. The number of strikes is increasing while their average duration, until fairly recently at least, has been tending to fall, indicating that industrial disputes are becoming more widespread and playing a more regular role in the collective bargaining process. More important, the increased frequency of strikes reflects a tendency towards local, as distinct from industry-wide, bargaining.

Collective bargaining has certainly increased inflationary pressures in the non-competitive sector of the economy although, as we have already seen, there is some doubt about the extent to which wage demands have been an independent cause of inflation. One important element in the role of collective bargaining in the inflationary process (and the more general push of rising expectations that lies behind it) has been the erosion of the relationship between increases in incomes and increases in productivity. Trade-union power has been used to prevent any downward movements in money wages at all; it has also been used to maintain and sometimes to narrow differentials, but always by upward movements. Any increases due to market forces pushing up wages in industries where labour is scarce and profits high, as

	Income from employment	Rent	Income from self-employment, profits and mixed incomes
1860–69	49	14	38
1900–1909	48	11	40
1920–29	60	7	34
1930–39	62	9	29
1948–57	72	4	24

SOURCE: Phyllis Deane and W. A. Cole, *British Economic Growth 1688–1959*, Cambridge University Press, 1969

Table 12: Shares in the National Income in the United Kingdom

Per cent

	Employers	Self-employed		Employees	Labour force
1911	4·6	12·8	8·2	87·2	100·0
1921	3·8	10·1	6·3	89·9	100·0
1931	n.a.	n.a.	6·1	n.a.	100·0
1951	2·2	7·2	5·0	92·8	100·0
1960		7·0		93·0	100·0
1965		6·5		93·5	100·0
1970		7·4		92·6	100·0
1973		7·8		92·2	100·0

SOURCE: As for table 11, and *Department of Employment Gazette*, HMSO

Table 13: Distribution of the Labour Force Between Employers, the Self-employed and Employees

in the motor industry in the 1950s and early 1960s, tend, by this ratchet effect, to bring other wages up with them.

Until the introduction of price control, larger companies were able to pass on the increase in wages in excess of increase in output per man by raising prices to the consumer. Smaller companies have been less able to do this because competition typically prevents them, and their less unionized employees have not been able to achieve as fast an increase in money earnings as their colleagues in larger companies. To some extent, therefore, the increase in incomes achieved by the unions has been at the expense of non-unionized employees. There is also evidence that average earnings of the self-employed are increasing less rapidly than those of employed persons.

There is more doubt about the extent to which unions have increased the share of wages and salaries in the national income at the expense of profits. It is true that the figures in Table 12 show that the share of income from employment has risen very sharply since the second half of the last century, but to a great extent this is the result of the shift from small to big business which has led to a massive decline in the numbers of self-employed. Table 13 illustrates this and shows that the process has been reversed since the 1960s.

Post-war data on the national income readily allow a more detailed breakdown of what are called 'factor incomes'. They show a downward trend in the share of company profits, which had declined (even after deducting stock appreciation[1]) to an all-time low of 40 per cent of 1952 levels by 1973, when government controls on prices accentuated a cyclical downturn in profitability. There was also a substantial increase in the share of public corporations and other public trading-enterprises, despite the effects of price controls and policies which depressed the returns earned by state enterprise, especially after 1969. The decline in the share of rent indicated in Table 12

---

1. Corporate profits are exaggerated under inflation by increases in the values of their stocks of raw materials and work in progress. Until some relief was given in the 1974 Finance Act, the whole of this increase in stocks was treated as taxable profit. Recent research, however, does not reveal any clear secular tendency for profits *after* tax to decline thanks to a declining effective corporate tax rate, hence the doubts expressed above.

did not continue and was in fact sharply reversed, but this is because the official statistics for rent include income imputed to the increasing numbers of owner-occupiers.

The world economy

This is a book primarily about Britain, but the broad trends we have been describing in this chapter are common to all the advanced countries. Some of them are to be found also in the developing countries, although for obvious reasons they are manifest there in very different ways.

I showed at the beginning of this chapter that massive increases in wealth have occurred in all the advanced countries over the last century, and this has been accompanied by a great increase in the role of the state. According to one measure of the role of the state in the economy – the ratio of final consumption expenditure by government to that by the private sector – it is very roughly of equal relative importance in the UK, Germany and the United States. The state is more important in Sweden than in the UK, and considerably less important in France and Japan; but its role is increasing everywhere.

The concentration of the private sector into larger and larger companies is again similar in the UK and the United States. It is probably much less concentrated in Germany and even less so in France, but concentration appears to be increasing in all these countries and in all other advanced countries for which any information is available. Increasing trade-union membership and readiness to take strike action is also familiar in all these countries.

The forces bringing about these changes and the mechanisms by which they are occurring seem to be similar in all countries, and because nations in the world economy are becoming more interdependent the changes are self-reinforcing. The money value of world trade tripled between 1960 and 1972 and this has increased the extent to which inflation is transmitted from country to country, just as increased trade has contributed to world economic growth. Particularly striking in this period was the projection at an international level of the concentration of economic activity and initiative into the hands of government, large private-sector organizations and, to a lesser extent, trade unions.

Many of the largest companies in the private sector have thus long since outgrown their national boundaries; the growth of the multinational enterprise has been one of the most dynamic elements in the world economy in the last two decades. These enterprises now account for around a quarter of total world trade and this share is increasing. The growth of the multinational enterprise has been accompanied by the development of international trade unions (or rather federations of trade unions), but this development, although important, has not yet been extensive and strike action in one country in support of employees in another, although not unknown, is still a relatively rare occurrence.

The state has also outgrown its economic boundaries and is now also becoming an international phenomenon. This has taken three forms. First of all some state enterprises have, like their private-sector counterparts, become multinational: examples are the state oil companies and airlines of many countries and the state-owned motor companies of Italy and France. Second, countries have tended to group together into blocs for the purpose or freer trade between them, or in order to exercise greater bargaining-power on a world scale, or both. In the EEC these objectives have been extended to include the establishment of political union also. Finally, states have set up inter-governmental agencies such as the IMF, the OECD and the United Nations to pursue common objectives, and have delegated powers to them. It is interesting that the IMF, originally conceived in 1944 to help maintain fixed exchange rates, except where fundamental disequilibria existed, is now creating units of 'paper gold' called SDRs.[1] These are accepted among members in settlement of international debts in much the same way as individual governments print money domestically. The declared purpose of issuing SDRs was to prevent a shortage of world liquidity which would hamper the growth of world trade, but they also help to avoid the necessity for contraction of spending in line with income in

1. Special Drawing Rights (SDRs) are valued in terms of a 'basket' of currencies and allocated to members in proportion to their quotas in the fund. Members agree to exchange SDRs for their own currencies on demand up to a limit of three times the allocation.

countries which have deficits on their current balances of payments. New initiatives in international cooperation are now being taken to deal with the problems created by the surpluses of the oil-producing countries, which are the counterpart of large trade deficits of the oil-importing countries brought about by the increase in oil prices that took place in 1973–4.

The developing countries

The developing countries as a group are very disparate and generalizations can be misleading, but contrary to popular impression they, as well as Western countries, have seen in the last century exceptional increases in consumption per head by historical standards. Increases in national wealth per head in the developing countries have been less rapid and more uneven than those in the advanced countries, but as a group they have made rapid progress, particularly since 1950. Average incomes, of course, remain very low, being measured in terms of a very few hundred dollars per head or even less, compared with the several thousand dollars per head by which we calculate incomes in the advanced countries (see pages 107–8).

Within these countries, and between countries within the group, the gains of faster economic growth have been unevenly shared. Thus income per head in Taiwan has grown exceptionally rapidly, while in Sri Lanka it has grown only relatively slowly. For some of the poorer countries virtually no reliable statistics are available at all and, in several, famine, war and natural disasters have resulted in negative growth for long periods. Within countries not much is known about income distribution but it is clear that those working in the new sectors of the economy, such as manufacturing industry or commodity processing, have benefited most, while those in the agricultural subsistence sectors have benefited least. Most of these countries are now self-governing, if in some instances heavily dependent upon aid. The pre-war influence of the colonial powers has virtually disappeared, so that a rapidly growing community of administrators and industrial and commercial employees with rapidly rising standards of living and education does exist in even the most backward of the developing countries. It is this group that predominates in the formation of economic and social policies.

Freedom from the control of the colonial powers and rising incomes, however unevenly shared, have therefore led to a widening of horizons in the developing countries which is in many respects having similar effects to those of the rising tide of wealth and political freedom in the advanced countries. The role of the state in the modern sectors of many of these countries is, in fact, greater than in most advanced countries. In some industries and in some countries multinational corporations also play a major role.

The enormous and growing gap between living standards in the advanced and developing countries and the relatively small and (at least until the early 1970s) declining share of the developing countries in world trade has in these circumstances stimulated economic nationalism in the developing world. This means that the concentration of economic initiative and power seen in the West is also increasingly prominent among the developing countries. Joint ventures between the state and multinational corporations in these countries, the growth of inter-government organizations such as ASEAN and OPEC, and the gradual emergence of the exercise of power as a group by the developing countries in the United Nations and its specialized agencies such as UNCTAD, are examples of this trend. The exercise of group bargaining-power by the Arab-Oil Exporting Countries in UAPEC is the most spectacular manifestation of the process I am describing, but it will undoubtedly be followed by others.

8. The Monetarists and the Keynesians

The General Theory

Chapter 6 superficially sketched the basic mechanism of inflation, boom and slump, but it left many questions unanswered and, in particular, left the impression that economists do not understand this mechanism fully and therefore are not likely to have an agreed diagnosis or prescription for our present difficulties. This is in fact so. There are two main schools of thought among economists and they are both direct descendants of the two views briefly mentioned in Chapter 6 – that of Keynes and that of the classical economists.[1] This time, however, it is the neo-Keynesians (for his thought has since been developed and extended, and some think distorted) who dominate the economic establishment and the neo-classicists who are in the minority. In addition, as the reader will have gathered from the previous chapter, the economic world is very different now from what it was in the 1930s.

To understand the debate it is necessary to know something of the contribution which Keynes made in the 1930s and how his views on unemployment differed from those of the classical economists, which gave support to the conventional wisdom of the time. The reader is warned that, although the conclusion is simple enough, full understanding of the arguments involved requires some intellectual effort.

Keynes approached his subject not so much in a different way from the classical economists as from a different direction. He was

1. I have not attempted to deal with the views of a new and influential group of economists, the Cambridge Economic Policy Group. They have particular views about the methods of economic management which should be adopted, particularly in so far as the scale of government borrowing affects the balance of payments. The Cambridge School are a Keynesian splinter group and their approach does not affect the basic conclusion of this chapter.

principally concerned with the relationships between four economic aggregates: total savings, investment, output and income and the factors that make them change. He developed a simple model for describing the national economy in which levels of output and employment are determined by the amounts which people decide to consume and firms decide to invest. The basis of his approach can be readily summarized. Output, in the short run at least, determines employment, since a given number of people will be required to produce any given level of production. Output is also the same thing as income, since the country as a whole (ignoring such complications as foreign trade) earns as much as it produces. In turn the country must either consume its output or invest it (that is, add to its ability to produce more in the future). This investment can take the form either of creating machines and other capital equipment or of storing the output in the form of inventories. Since the decisions to produce, whether for consumer or investment goods, are taken by one set of people (firms) while the decisions to spend income on consumption now or to save it for the future are taken by another set of people (households), it is clear that the two sets of decisions will not necessarily balance one another.

Keynes's General Theory was a theory of how these aggregates are, in fact, brought into equilibrium. He showed that although the decisions of people to save and firms to invest are made quite independently of one another, actual savings and investment are brought into equality primarily by changing the level of output and income. Thus, if firms are planning to invest more than people desire to save, the national income will increase and this larger income will allow savings to rise and match investment. This apparently miraculous adjustment comes about through the effects of the multiplier which I described briefly in Chapter 6. An increase in investment expenditure, an expansion in orders for new machines, say, increases incomes and employment in the machine-tool industry as new labour is engaged. Increased spending by those employed in that industry leads to higher incomes in consumer-goods industries, and so on. In fact, the greater the proportion of their income which people spend and the smaller the proportion saved, the greater will be this multiplier sequence: that is to say, the greater will be the total increase in incomes resulting from an initial increase in investment expenditure. But, at each stage of the process – as the effects fan out from the machine-tool industry – money will be saved out of the increased incomes, and these increases in savings will accumulate until what people want to save is equal to what businessmen are investing. It is only at this point that the system is in equilibrium, meaning that there is no necessity for change because savings will equal investment or, more generally, planned output by firms will match the planned expenditure of households. This mechanism, the reader will remember from Chapter 6, works in reverse, too, so that if, for example, individuals decide to save more than businessmen wish to invest, their lower current spending will bring down incomes and output to the point where savings fall to equal the amount invested.

This is, of necessity, a simplified explanation of the process. In actual situations things would be much more complicated than this: incomes and output or investment might not be able to respond to changes in decisions about how much to save or invest without considerable lags; but Keynes's analysis had nonetheless very clear and important implications for employment. Since the level of incomes determines the level of employment it follows that employment is determined by the amounts which businessmen decide to invest and which individuals decide to save (or consume). There is no reason, Keynes showed, why these decisions should result in equilibrium at a level of output which would achieve full employment. He believed that the prolonged unemployment of the 1930s was the result of equilibrium in fact being achieved at a level of output far below the full-employment level. This was why he advocated that governments should invest in public works. Such spending would result in increases in incomes through the multiplier and raise employment. What the individual consumer or businessman would not do, the government would do for them.

Keynes also believed that the government should do what it could to bring interest rates down by appropriate monetary policies, because lower interest rates would make it cheaper for businessmen to borrow money and would tend to stimulate investment. He did not think, however, that interest rates were likely to fall far enough to be effective.

Keynes and the classics

The reader should now be in a position to understand the basis of Keynes's case for increased public spending. The classical economists advocated not public spending but policies to bring down interest rates and wages, to stimulate increased investment and business activity. They feared that increased government expenditure would simply delay or even frustrate the changes that had to take place in the economy before growth and full employment could be restored. Keynes's case was, in essence, that reducing wages would make matters worse. Simply reducing expenditure would reduce income still further, while reducing interest rates, though helpful, could not of itself be guaranteed to be effective.

It should not be thought, however, that Keynes won the theoretical argument. Professor Pigou (whose exposition of classical macro-economics[1] was taken by Keynes as the false theory which he had to rebut) was able to show that, even on Keynes's own assumptions, falling prices would lead eventually to a self-correcting upward movement in demand, output and employment if the system was allowed to work. His argument was, in effect, that as prices fell the real purchasing power of cash and other liquid balances in the hands of the public would increase. This increase in real wealth would eventually lead to more spending and set in train the upward movement needed to expand output and restore full employment.

Although not susceptible to conclusive proof the Pigou effect is theoretically sustainable, and it could be argued that it did play a part in the slow underlying recovery in output that took place during the middle 1930s. An objection to reliance on Pigou's theory in support of a policy for allowing prices to decline as a 'cure' for a slump is that it does seem that considerable time, perhaps several years, would have to elapse before the increased real wealth resulting from falling prices would be translated into higher incomes.

---

1. This term, which refers to the study of aggregates such as income and employment, as distinct from micro-economics which focuses upon individual decision units such as firms, was not used at the time.

In 1939 the war came along, however, and the increased government expenditure that came with it brought in Keynesian policies without any overt revolution in official economic thought. Until much later, therefore, the controversy was overtaken by events. It was only in the early 1960s, when the problem of persistently rising prices was forced upon the attention of economists, that the issue was resurrected, but then it was in the quite different circumstances of concern about inflation and full employment rather than about depression and unemployment.

Much effort, typewriter ribbon and letterpress has since been spent, especially in the last decade or so, on trying to analyse exactly what Keynes's contribution to economics was. His policies were put into effect through the pressure of events and this would have happened even if *The General Theory* had never been written. Further work on his technical analysis (whether it is described as neo-classical or neo-Keynesian) has blurred the distinction between Keynesian and classical thought. It is now suggested, for example, that Keynes's technical innovations, his emphasis on aggregates and the impetus they gave to the development of macro-economics have mainly helped to rationalize what has happened rather than, as is usually supposed, being instrumental in bringing it about. The important issue remaining in dispute in the macro-economics of employment is that of the role of the money supply. Before I move on to this, however, I want to try briefly to explain more precisely why the course of events described in the previous chapter, then at a relatively early stage, may have left the technical argument about the self-correcting mechanism behind.

It may well be that a more rapid decline in wages and prices would have stimulated a more rapid recovery in the 1930s, but it was not only resistance on the part of trade unions that prevented this from occurring. Other forces were at work to modify, if not to invalidate, the classical theory which had largely been worked out during the nineteenth century, when the structure of the economy was very different from what it had become by the inter-war period.

Not only were trade unions more powerful in the 1930s than in the 1870s, but there had been changes in the predominant types of firms which employed labour. Owner-managed businesses operating in fragmented and highly competitive markets were giving way to state enterprise and larger public companies which exercised considerable influence over their market environment. This change affected the self-correcting mechanism in two ways. First, these large companies were able to resist downward movements in their product prices; and second, the separation of the ownership from the control of businesses meant that decisions about savings and investment were also increasingly separate. In an owner-managed business, a textile mill for example, the mill-owner would tend to plough his savings into his own business rather than invest in other businesses, so that savings tended to be automatically invested. Keynes's argument that there was no mechanism to ensure that excess savings could not lead to declines in incomes would have had little force in these earlier circumstances. These factors help to explain why the self-correcting mechanism of the business cycle could be expected to be weaker in the 1930s than in earlier periods, although the differences are of degree rather than of kind.

Keynes's thought was rooted in a particular stage in economic development, the Great Depression. His theory was essentially a short-term analysis aimed at breaking out of mass unemployment and not at inflation as a long-term problem. In fact, he thought that the world economy would exhibit a persistent tendency to depression through lack of investment. It has indeed been repeatedly pointed out that the General Theory is not a general theory at all, omitting as it does any analysis of some of the important dynamic problems of employment, investment and growth.

Keynes and inflation

Our present economic problems are different from those of the 1930s, and the changes in the economy that have taken place since then again require a new approach. Keynes's pre-war policy prescriptions are of little help now. Such advice as he gave on dealing with inflation, as in his How to Pay for the War, appears to be based on the assumption that it would be a temporary problem resulting from excess demand and one that could be dealt with by fiscal policy, that is by mopping up purchasing power through a budget surplus fed by higher taxation and physical controls. He did not envisage a situation in which the control of inflation and prevention of chronic unemployment call for conflicting policy measures. This is the dilemma we appear to face today.

After the Second World War Keynesians for the most part believed that fine tuning of the economy should be sufficient to keep price increases at a moderate level (they believed that a *gently* increasing price-level was conducive to economic growth). When inflationary pressures became excessive it was necessary only to operate Keynesian policies in reverse, that is, to reduce government expenditure and to increase taxes. By the early 1960s, however, it became clear that this policy was not sufficient to keep prices in check while maintaining a reasonable level of employment. It was also obvious, in Britain in particular, that economic forecasting of an unattainably accurate kind was necessary to 'fine tune' in this way. So difficult is it, in fact, to foresee an increase in inflationary pressure or a downturn in demand, and so complex are the lags in response to changes in policy, that many economists argue that government actions have, in practice, been de-stabilizing rather than stabilizing since the war.

Since that time there has been increasing agreement among Keynesians on the need for a prices and incomes policy to achieve price stability while leaving freedom to use changes in government spending to pursue full-employment policies. However, in Britain successive governments have failed to secure agreement for sustained policies to control incomes. Controls over prices have been imposed, but in the absence of any reduction in cost-increases these price controls have simply led to falling profit margins and investment, which by 1974 threatened to precipitate a liquidity crisis in the corporate sector.

The majority of economists can probably now be described as Keynesians in the sense that they accept the Keynesian interpretation of the short-term workings of the economy. A somewhat smaller majority probably also agree on the necessity for a prices and incomes policy which they see as the only answer to the dilemma of stag-flation. There are, of course, many differences of opinion about the relative extent to which excessive demand resulting from full-employment policies and rising costs from excessive wage demands are responsible for inflation. Some Keynesians consider that in the circumstances of the early 1970s there was excessive demand and that government spending should have been reduced.

Does money matter?

There is a minority of economists which fundamentally disagrees with the neo-Keynesian view: and these are the monetarists, a group of economists among which Milton Friedman of Chicago University is especially prominent. Although there are varying shades of view in the monetarist school, all its members attach great importance to the money supply in explaining not merely prices but economic output and employment as well.

The money supply (or the money stock as it is often called) is the quantity of money in the economy. Money, or purchasing power, which seems a simple enough thing to most of us, can be defined in several ways. It must of course include notes and coins in circulation, but current accounts at banks are also money and it is usual to include them. A wider definition of the money supply includes deposit accounts and this is the one used in Chart 7 and Table 14, which compare the growth in the money supply with growth in the national income and prices.

The monetarists accept that short-term changes in prices can occur for a variety of reasons, but maintain that continued inflation is always the result of an excess of the increase in money supply over increases in output. The basis of the monetarist view is the quantity theory of money which was developed by Irving Fisher in the United States right at the beginning of the twentieth century. The starting point of the theory is the Fisher equation: $MV = PT$, where M is the stock of money, V the velocity of circulation, P the average price level and T the flow of real goods and services. This may seem very technical, but it is fairly easily understood. The equation states that the total value of goods sold in the economy (PT) must equal the volume of finance available, which is given by the stock of money multiplied by the number of times it has circulated to finance the necessary transactions (MV).

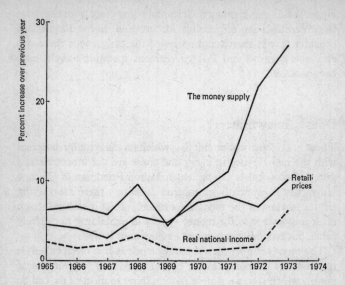

Chart 7: Annual Increases in Real National Income, Money Supply and Retail Prices in the UK, 1965-73.

SOURCE: see Table 14.

	Prices 1970 = 100	Percentage increase over previous year	Money supply M3 £ million	Percentage increase over previous year	National income £ million	Percentage increase over previous year		National income as ratio of money supply
						At current prices	At 1970 prices	
1964	75.3	—	11,376	—	26,854	—		2.4
1965	78.7	4.5	12,100	6.4	28,674	6.8	2.3	2.4
1966	81.9	4.1	12,919	6.8	30,275	5.6	1.6	2.3
1967	84.2	2.8	13,665	5.8	31,878	5.3	2.0	2.3
1968	88.9	5.6	14,978	9.6	34,015	6.7	3.2	2.3
1969	93.2	4.8	15,618	4.3	35,710	5.0	1.5	2.3
1970	100.0	7.3	16,930	8.4	39,019	9.3	1.3	2.3
1971	108.1	8.1	18,831	11.2	43,784	12.2	1.5	2.3
1972	115.4	6.8	22,941	21.8	48,962	11.8	1.8	2.1
1973	127.1	10.1	29,151	27.1	56,259	14.9	6.3	1.9

(The price index is the implied national income deflator, not the retail price index used elsewhere in the book.)

SOURCE: *National Income and Expenditure, 1963–73*, HMSO; and various issues of *Financial Statistics*

Table 14: Prices, the National Income and the Money Supply in the UK, 1964–73

This must be so, since the total money paid to settle transactions must necessarily be the same as the money value of the goods sold. The equation is, therefore, an identity: the left and right hand sides are the same thing.

As always in economics, things get more difficult when theory is translated into practice. In practice we do not know the total number or value of transactions in the economy, nor do we know the velocity of circulation. But we do have an estimate of the national income, which reflects the value of final transactions, so we can calculate what is called the income velocity of circulation. The number of transactions multiplied by their average price would obviously yield a figure which is very much bigger than the national income because most goods change hands several times on their journey from producer to final consumer. Income velocity is calculated by dividing the national income by the money stock. It can be seen from Table 14 that in 1973 the average money supply was £29,151 million and the national income was £56,259 million, so in that case the income velocity of circulation was 1·9.

Keynesian economists would accept all this, but what the monetarists have done is to go a step further and argue that the velocity of circulation is in fact fairly stable and that changes in the money supply (M in the equation) *cause* changes in the national income: that is, in terms of the equation, that an increase in M will cause an increase in PT. If there is unemployment the T (transactions) component can rise without any noticeable change in the price-level because output can increase; but if, at full employment, the money supply is increased, then the price-level will rise because more money will be chasing the same quantity of goods. They do not argue that these consequences follow immediately, or even with a constant lag, but that a change in the money supply will always result in a change in the money national income.

This is where Keynesians and monetarists part company, since Keynesians believe that changes in the national income are primarily the result of changes in expenditure (or saving) and they do not accept that changes in the supply of money will directly affect the volume of expenditure at all. They argue that increases in the supply of money will at most only affect expenditure indirectly through reducing the cost of borrowing. If this led to increased investment by business it would increase expenditure, and hence income, through the multiplier process already described. It is, however, generally agreed that investment is not particularly sensitive to the rate of interest, so that in practice the causal effects of increasing the money supply would be slight.

I have, to simplify exposition, left out a number of complicating factors, in particular those involved in determining the actual amounts of cash which people hold. I have also used the labels Keynesian and monetarist to group individuals whose views differ quite widely. For example, the followers of Keynes seem to have gone further than their master in minimizing the role of the quantity of money in the system. Nonetheless, the two schools of thought point in different directions. The Keynesians believe that changes in the quantity of money are not an important element in determining the level of demand and activity. They believe that additional money in the system will directly result only in a reduction in the velocity of circulation and will affect demand only via the rate of interest: in some conditions these effects will not be important. In contrast, the monetarists believe that the availability of more money will lead directly to an increase in expenditure, which will be reinforced by changes in interest rates. This increased expenditure will push prices up to the extent that goods are not available, and will only lead to an increase in activity to the extent that the necessary resources are available.

Why is it that such differing views cannot be resolved? Table 14 appears to bear out the monetarist thesis. Over the last decade the money supply has been increased at a much faster rate than the growth of real income, and this rate and the rate at which prices are increasing has been accelerating. There has also been a tendency for a speeding-up in the rate of increase in the money supply to be associated with a speeding-up of the increase in real income, and vice versa. The year-to-year correspondence of prices and income and money supply are not perfect; this could not be expected because of lags in the system. In particular, expectations about future price-changes affect those changes and take time to modify.

Historical research indicates that the association of the rate of growth of the money supply, real output and the price-level is universal. The 1921 decline in prices and employment, for example, was accompanied by an exceptional contraction in the money supply, and monetarists believe that monetary mismanagement was the true cause of the Great Depression.

A great deal of detailed work has been done to test the various relationships between the monetary system, its elements, and real output and prices, but it has been inconclusive. This is because statistical relationships do not prove *causality*. It can and has been argued by Keynesians that increased prices and incomes are the cause of increases in the money supply, and not the other way round as the monetarists claim. They argue that if prices rise as a result of pressure from increased costs, or through increased investment, the liquidity of the banking system will be reduced and interest rates will rise. The monetary authorities must allow the money supply to increase in order to prevent a liquidity crisis in industry which could cause many firms to go bankrupt and result in massive unemployment. But, argue the monetarists, it is excessive spending in monetary terms which is contributing to pressures on cost and prices. This could be avoided if the government raised taxes or borrowed from the public rather than expanding the money supply. If this policy of tight money were sustained, firms, trade unions and others would soon accept that they could not *finance* a sharp increase in the money value of transactions and, given the choice, would soon settle for a larger volume at stable prices rather than a reduced volume at higher prices. Once inflationary expectations were checked in this way, a tight money policy would, in fact, be helping to bring about price stability with full employment.

The politics of economics

The difference between Keynesian and monetarist views is clear enough in the circumstances of a major depression with stable or declining prices. What do these differences imply for the 1974-5 situation of record rates of inflation and increasing unemployment?

Crudely speaking, Keynesian analysis suggests that the problems of unemployment and inflation can be regarded as separate. Rising prices are the outcome of cost push resulting from excessive increases in incomes, but unemployment must be the result of inadequate demand. The Keynesian prescription, therefore, is for a policy to control increases in prices and incomes, accompanied by measures to expand demand to take up the unemployed resources in the economy. Reducing the money supply, the argument runs, would do nothing directly to reduce expenditure, wage demands or prices, although if pursued with sufficient vigour it could, through higher interest rates, lead to lower investment and corporate liquidity problems which would aggravate the unemployment problem.

The monetarists maintain for their part that incomes and prices policies simply *suppress* inflation instead of curing it, and result in gross distortions of the economic system. They believe that the problem will only be solved if the money supply ceases to grow faster than output. Since the monetarists believe changes in the money supply in relation to output work through to changes in expenditure, such action will directly reduce demand, and for this reason the rate of growth of the money supply should be brought down gradually to that of output.

Although the monetarist revival is relatively recent – it dates from the 1960s – one distinguished thinker, Professor Hayek, now in his middle seventies, has consistently argued against Keynes along these lines and indeed has been predicting the outset of stag-flation since the 1930s.

He argues that what Keynes was advocating was in effect to make the price-level change in relation to wage rates rather than the other way round, and that this device, like the efforts of the sorcerer's apprentice, has got out of hand. Securing higher employment has been gained simply by making activities appear in the result to be more profitable than they were expected to be, and by allowing people to expect that incomes, as well as prices, would be allowed to rise as necessary. This can only be done by an accelerating rate of inflation, since more and more types of activity become dependent upon inflation to remain viable. If inflation slows down then these activities cease to be viable and collapse. Professor Hayek's diagnosis is convincing and the accuracy of his predictions is impressive.

The dispute really comes back, therefore, to the same issue that was debated in the 1930s. After fifty years and more of a decentralized competitive system, the majority of economists then wanted to allow the market mechanism to work. Now, after fifty years of an increasingly centralized economic system, the majority of economists want to intervene by controlling prices and only a minority want to leave the market mechanism to do the job.

Whether consciously or not, the dispute between the Keynesians and the monetarists is ultimately about political rather than purely economic matters. The ways in which people's attitudes and expectations about inflation operate, and the ways in which they can be changed, are not simple, technical economic questions; they ultimately touch upon community and personal behaviour and upon the forms of government and economic discipline which people will accept. Seen in this light, the argument about the role of money is not merely a technical side-issue with few policy implications of practical importance. The Keynesian solution of prices and incomes policies inevitably means reducing the role of the price system in allocating labour and other resources, and this eventually must lead either to inefficiency or to central direction by the state (or both, according to your political persuasion).

The monetarists wish to return to a decentralized economy and their prescriptions are consistent with this desire; the Keynesians, in preferring incomes and price control, are pointing in the opposite direction and, as the previous chapter demonstrated, they are pointing in the direction in which we are moving.

9. What Economists do not Know

The evolving economic system

It is now time to draw together the arguments of this second part of the book. Rising affluence following the diffusion and development of the industrial revolution in technology and industrial organization has led to increased demands for freedom and security. This in turn has led to a massive extension in the role of the state and a parallel concentration of the private sector into larger and larger units of organization, affecting employers through corporations and employees through trade unions. This whole process has been self-reinforcing and is still continuing.

At the beginning of the period we have been looking at, the economic system was very decentralized: individual consumers voted with their purchasing power for goods and services which were supplied by large numbers of relatively small firms, none of which could exert significant influence over its market, and which were obliged to follow the signals given by the price mechanism. The same mechanism operated not only in final consumer and capital goods markets, but also in the market for labour and, in a more complex way, in the market for capital. This was the system upon which classical economics was built: the economics of the competitive system.

The modern system, by contrast, is highly centralized. Economic resources are increasingly allocated through the exercise of bargaining power between the state, organized labour and large corporations. Overlapping these groups are other organizations – consumer, employer and special interest groups. Thus, the new system is one that requires an understanding not only of the economics of competition but also of the economics of power. Many detailed changes have occurred which have modified the mechanism through which the economic system operates: for example, corporations can exert considerable influence, through sales promotion and the control of retail outlets, over the quantities, prices and characteristics of the goods and services they supply.

The evolution of the economic system in this way has been accompanied and reinforced by subtle changes in economic objectives. Thus, corporations no longer single-mindedly pursue profit: this has been replaced by a set of more complex objectives including growth and security. The security of companies, it is now recognized, requires the pursuit of the interests of its employees and the general public as well as of its shareholders. Trade unions are increasingly concerned with obtaining payment by the hour rather than by physical work done (piece rates), and with redundancy payments and other protection against loss of earnings. The proportion of the labour force being paid by salary rather than wages is steadily increasing.

The picture is confused by the fact that a major remnant of the old economic order survives alongside the new. Small firms, whose employees (if any) are not unionized and which can exert little or no control over their markets, continue to account for between about a quarter and a half of the labour force in the advanced countries. These firms are, on the whole, not engaged in the same activities as the giant corporations: they are concerned mainly with supplying services, including professional and artistic services, or with manufacturing activities requiring great flexibility or little capital. The continued existence of these survivors from the old order does not alter the basic direction of economic development, which has so far clearly been towards increased centralization, although it does mean that the private sector of the economy must be regarded as having two parts, each of which functions differently.

The economics of competition

Modern economics has yet to assimilate these changes fully and there are wide differences of opinion about the extent to which classical economics, which was developed when the economic system was much more decentralized than it is now, is helpful in explaining what is happening now. For it is undoubtedly true that, although they have been developed and extended in many ways, the analytical method and many of the doctrines held by the majority of economists are still basically those of classical economics. The so-called Keynesian revolution did clear away some of the almost theological justifications for profit and saving which were deeply embedded in classical thought and help to provide an apparently ideology-free justification for more state intervention in economic affairs. But Keynes did not offer any assistance at all in explaining how the working of the economic system would be affected in the longer run by increased state intervention. We are still trying to grapple with this, for the most part with the tools of classical economics.

In the classical system, resources of land, labour and capital were allocated by the price mechanism, and the way in which economic activity was organized was itself determined by the same mechanism. Changes in relative prices and the changes in profitability that they brought about channelled resources into those activities which gave maximum consumer satisfaction at least cost. As time went by it was increasingly recognized that there were frictions and imperfections – such as instances of monopoly – in the system, but on the whole this was how it worked.

To the extent that individuals and corporate enterprise still have discretionary power over the way they spend their incomes and the way they respond in their own economic activities to the spending of others, the price mechanism is still working. The efficient functioning of this mechanism was always a matter of degree, if only because there would have to be perfect knowledge – of a clairvoyant kind – in the market place for it to work perfectly. For example, a manufacturer would have to know at what level he would have to set his prices to sell his output of goods before he put them on the market, and all consumers would have to be aware of what was on the market if misallocation of resources was to be avoided.

The economics of power

In the modern economy, however, individuals do not have full discretion over how their incomes are spent: the state spends much of it for them. State spending is allocated not by the price mechanism (although it is influenced by it) but by what politicians believe people want, or think they should want. Companies no longer have to take market demand as given; they can influence it to a considerable extent. Incomes and profits are not determined solely by the free working of the price-mechanism; they are also greatly influenced by the bargaining power of trade unions, the market power of companies and the policies of government. However much it may be the social will that is ultimately responsible for the modification of the economic system in this way, it is obvious that the democratic vote is a less sensitive instrument for allocating resources in detail than the price mechanism. It is also obvious that as the decentralized system is dismantled more and more of its functions must be absorbed into the state.

Even at the stage which has been reached today, the process has quite radical implications for our understanding of the economic system and our ability to assess what is happening now, as well as to predict events in the future. Economic statistics, for example, are much more difficult to interpret under contemporary conditions than in the competitive situation underlying classical thought. The GNP is now quite widely recognized as being a very imperfect indicator of welfare because it does not allow for many social costs, such as atmospheric pollution, and excludes the contribution to welfare of unpaid persons such as housewives. It is less generally appreciated that economic statistics of this kind are very difficult to interpret anyway, except under competitive conditions. Indeed, it is not at all clear what the GNP means under contemporary conditions. If the government employs a thousand more tax inspectors, or if a large corporation doubles its advertising budget to persuade the public of its concern over pollution, then GNP rises (if these resources were previously unemployed), but it is not obvious that welfare has increased. Unless consumers *want* what is being produced and are prepared to pay for it, how can it contribute to welfare?

To take another example, the capital market in the classical system allocated savings to productive investment according to the profitability of that investment, and that profitability indicated that the price mechanism was drawing resources in response to consumer demand. In the early part of the nineteenth century this came about directly because the proprietors of profitable companies tended to re-invest their savings in their own businesses. Later on, the capital market became more specialized and sophisticated and the users of capital bid in the market for savings via the rate of interest they paid on stock or the dividends paid on shares. Today (to simplify) neither the users of capital nor the suppliers are connected through the price mechanism in the same way. Much investment is made by government out of tax revenue; much more is made through the re-invested earnings of companies: in neither case is the investor bidding for funds in the capital market. The bulk of individual savings are now made in a more or less automatic fashion through life-insurance premiums, social-security and pension-fund contributions, and these funds are invested for institutions by persons for whom security and other non-economic objectives may, as we have seen, take precedence over profit.

It is impossible to say precisely what the implications of the change from competitive economics to the economics of power are for economic growth, the returns on different kinds of economic activity, savings, prices and employment. My view of the immediate outlook is given in Chapter 1. There are some aspects of it upon which a high probability can be placed, such as the continuation of high rates of inflation, and in this I may be vindicated by events; but much of what will happen will, as in the past, be a surprise to most people, including economists.

It must be admitted that there are many matters even among past events upon which economics throws little light. Because of this economists are frequently compared unfavourably with their colleagues in the physical sciences. This is unfair. Economics is more difficult than physical science because the subject matter is changing all the time and because at any given time it is rarely possible to conduct controlled experiments. For example, in the dispute over the role of the money supply in inflation the direction of causality could be either way, but other events will not stand still while lengthy experiments are carried out to test alternative theories.

Even if the Keynesians are right, however, and the only solution to the problem of inflation is the control of incomes and prices, it is clear that more and more state intervention will be required to take over the role of the price mechanism in allocating resources and maintaining employment. Even if the monetarists are right and inflation could be moderated, if not eliminated, simply by gradually controlling the money supply, it is doubtful whether in contemporary circumstances, without other measures to restore the competitive system, the price mechanism could work effectively to re-allocate resources without severe dislocation, including very high and prolonged levels of unemployment. Either way, therefore, we stand on the threshold of further major changes in social and economic organization.

Notes on Further Reading

'Life is short and the number of books is appalling.'
(John Cowper Powys, *The Meaning of Culture*)

Introduction

The few who argue for a return to smaller-scale units of economic
activity are generally regarded as cranks, although the idea is a
little more respectable now than it was in 1971 when my book,
The Juggernauts, first appeared. E. F. Schumacher, whose col-
lection of essays, *Small is Beautiful* (Blond & Briggs, 1973), has
clearly struck a chord in the public mind, now advocates the use of
what he calls 'intermediate technology', even in the advanced
countries, to create employment and increase job satisfaction. A
programme of economic policy for decentralizing economic
activity and restoring the functions of the price mechanism is set
out in *The Intelligent Radical's Guide to Economic Policy*, by
James Meade (George Allen & Unwin, 1975).

Chapter 1

This chapter only attempts to give the most general perspective on
the economic outlook. The interested reader should keep up to
date by reading the newspapers and can re-check continually in the
regular reviews of the National Institute of Social and Economic
Research and in the OECD *Economic Outlook*, which appears
each July and December.

Chapter 2

It is important to keep abreast of changes in tax and other matters
affecting income and employment. This can be done by reading
the papers or taking professional advice. The Inland Revenue is
happy to answer questions and this service is free; but they will
not take the initiative, you have to do that yourself. Your local

social security office will give advice on state contributions and pensions.

The onset of the recession resulted in a boom in books on gardening, home wine-making, brewing, and self-sufficiency generally. For those who are serious, or just enjoy reading about it, I particularly recommend *Self-Sufficiency*, by John and Sally Seymour (Faber & Faber, 1973). The Penguin book, *Home Brewing and Wine-Making* is exceptionally good. Electricity showrooms have books on freezing, and I won't go into gardening at all. You are on your own there.

Chapters 3 and 5

Easily the best 'how-to-do' book on stock-exchange investment that I know of is *The Art and Practice of Investment*, by W. G. Nursaw (Hutchinson, third edition, 1974). An elementary and sound, if uncritical, book on stock-exchange investment which also covers taxation, house purchase and insurance is *The Save and Prosper Book of Money* (Collins, revised edition, 1974). A much more advanced, though already rather dated, book for the more affluent which also covers death duties, investment abroad and other higher states of the art is *The Creation and Protection of Capital*, edited by Oliver Stanley (Sweet & Maxwell, 1974). There are lots of books about taxation, including, I believe, a good annual one by Hambros Bank, but I've not read any of them. There is little yet available for the general reader on indexation: *Monetary Correction*, by Milton Friedman (Institute of Economic Affairs, 1974), gives a brief introduction to the subject and contains a bibliography. The Financial Times Ltd will publish an Economists' Advisory Group study on indexation (by E. Victor Morgan and others) during 1975.

Chapter 4

I used *The World of Gold Today*, by Timothy Green (White Lion, 1974), for much of the background to this chapter and it contains a good bibliography. The annual review, *Gold 1974*, by

Peter D. Fells (Consolidated Gold Fields), was my source for the statistics on production and demand for gold. The *Annual Bullion Review* published by Samuel Montagu and the *Monthly Market Report* published by Sharps Pixley were my sources for monthly prices of bullion and coin premia, and are worth reading for those who want to follow events in world gold markets. *The Destiny of Gold*, by Paul Einzig (Macmillan, 1972), is a good introduction to the monetary role of gold, although the late author (I suspect inadvertently) assumes quite a lot of knowledge in his readers.

The American books on becoming rich referred to in this chapter, and an additional one, are: *How to Make Money Fast Speculating in Distressed Property*, by John Kamin (Pyramid Books, 1973); *How You Can Profit from the Coming Devaluation*, by Harry Browne (Avon Books, 1971); *How You Can Profit from a Monetary Crisis*, by Harry Browne (Macmillan Publishing, New York, 1974); *Panics and Crashes and How You Can Make Money Out of Them*, by Harry D. Schultz (Business Books, London, 1974). I would only really recommend Browne to the addict of this type of literature.

Chapter 6

Most intermediate text-books on economics describe our understanding of business cycles. There are many specialized books on the subject, though none that I know of is intended for the general reader. For a general text-book of economics I like *Economics, An Introductory Analysis*, by Paul A. Samuelson (McGraw-Hill, 1974). Samuelson has made major contributions to trade-cycle theory and his section on this is very good. His text-book is a reliable guide to the whole corpus of contemporary theory, though it is inevitably a bit 'square' on some controversial issues dealt with in this book. There is a very readable chapter on the trade cycle in *The General Theory of Employment, Interest and Money*, by J. M. Keynes (Macmillan, 1973); and those who wish to pursue the development of later work could start by following up the references given under 'Trade cycle' in the *Penguin Dictionary of Economics*, by G. Bannock, R. E. Baxter and R. Rees (1972). I naturally recommend the *Penguin Dictionary* to the general reader who gets stuck on any of the terms or concepts introduced in this book, or even, in many instances, where he wants signposts to follow a topic through further.

A scholarly but comprehensive book on the British economy between the wars, which incorporates the results of recent research, is *The Inter-War Economy: Britain 1919–1939*, by D. H. Aldcroft (B. T. Batsford, 1970). It contains an extensive bibliography. A less up-to-date though easier-to-read book with a more international perspective is *Economic Survey, 1919–1939*, by W. A. Lewis (George Allen & Unwin, 1949).

Chapters 7 and 9

Contemporary thought on the economics of power is, of course, dominated by the work of J. K. Galbraith, whose books are clear *and* entertaining as well as major contributions to thought. *The New Industrial State* (second edition, André Deutsch, 1972; Penguin Books, 1974) and *Economics and the Public Purpose* (Penguin Books, 1975) must be read by anyone interested in the subject of these two chapters. The second book of the two mentioned is the more important, but has so far received much less attention.

While Galbraith sees concentration of power as a technological necessity and socialism as the only means of mitigating its effects, I see it simply as an outcome of economic progress and political bargaining. The problem is not a new one. Marx expected socialism to come through revolution, but J. A. Schumpeter in *Capitalism, Socialism and Democracy* (George Allen & Unwin, 1943) foresaw, more correctly it now seems, the likelihood of a peaceful evolution. H. A. Hayek in *The Road to Serfdom* (Routledge & Kegan Paul, 1944) has traced the way in which state intervention is self-reinforcing and how it threatens democratic freedom. The link between rising wealth and the process of integrative change in social institutions, and its implications, has been developed by Joe Roeber in *The Organisation in a Changing Environment* (Addison-Wesley, Reading, Massachusetts, 1973) and I have drawn heavily upon that. For some brief discussion of the interactions between the growth of business concentration, the capital market and the decline in the importance of small firms see 'A New Look at the Growth of Industrial Concentration', by S. J. Prais (Oxford Economic Papers, July 1974). I have traced some of the qualitative effects of international business concentration and the development of thought and statistical research on the subject in *The Juggernauts* (Penguin, 1973).

The sources of the facts on the centralization of our economic institutions are for the most part given in the notes to the tables in Chapter 7. Particularly important are, *The UK Economy*, *A Manual of Applied Economics*, edited by A. R. Prest and D. J. Coppock (Weidenfeld & Nicolson, fifth edition, 1974), a valuable general source; *British Economic Growth 1688–1959*, by P. Deane and W. A. Cole (Cambridge University Press, 1962); and *Economic Growth in the West*, by Angus Maddison (George Allen & Unwin, 1964). Angus Maddison's *Economic Progress and Policy in the Developing Countries* (George Allen & Unwin, 1970) was also an important source for the section on developing countries.

Very few books on the economics of power illustrate their arguments with statistics. One exception is *British Capitalism, Workers and the Profits Squeeze*, by Andrew Glyn and Bob Sutcliffe (Penguin, 1972), which contains good, though sometimes very misleading, statistical analysis in a neo-Marxist setting. For a recent and more balanced view on corporate profitability in particular, see 'The UK Profits Crisis: Myth or Reality ?', by M. A. King (*Economic Journal*, March 1975). A good general and non-technical exposition of an institutional view of inflation is *Inflation: A World-Wide Disaster*, by Irving S. Friedman (Hamish Hamilton, 1973). Hard evidence on the contribution of concentrated industries to inflation and a survey of inflation in several countries is contained in an important new book, *The Roots of Inflation*, by Gardiner C. Means and others (Wilton House Publications Ltd., 1975). Those interested in institutional economics (an alternative term to the economics of power) and in the problems of scientific method and the language in which economists work should read Gunnar Myrdal, starting with *Against the Stream* (Macmillan, 1974). Galbraith's *The New Industrial State*, already mentioned, is also good on this.

Chapter 8

Keynes and After, by Michael Stewart (Penguin Books, 1970), goes
as deeply into the subject-matter of this chapter as most general
readers would want to go, and the book is a singular achievement
in clarity and readability. It was written before the more recent
disenchantment with Keynesian policies set in and does not, in any
event, do full justice to the monetarist case, but it is well worth
reading. The daring reader who wishes to go further should read
Keynes's *General Theory* (detailed in the section on Chapter 6)
himself. Much of it is not easy going but quite a lot is a delight to
read, and better and clearer, than most of the writings of the neo-
Keynesians. It might be as well for the less confident to read
Samuelson (op. cit.) on the subject before tackling the master
himself. Sir John Hicks's three very important lectures (upon
which I have drawn) in *The Crisis in Keynesian Economics* (Basil
Blackwell, 1974) are helpful in putting Keynes's thought in its
contemporary perspective as well as advancing it. Indeed, anyone
who wants to understand Keynes should also read Hicks's earlier
interpretations of Keynes in *Critical Essays in Monetary Theory*,
by John Hicks (Oxford University Press, 1967). The political
implications of Keynes's work are illuminated in *Economic
Philosophy*, by Joan Robinson (The New Thinker's Library,
C. A. Watts, 1962). The general reader should not be deterred by
the title of this book: it is beautifully clear and very short. *Essays
on John Maynard Keynes*, edited by Milo Keynes (Cambridge
University Press, 1975), contains a very clear summary of
Keynes's General Theory by James Meade, a monetarist assessment of Keynes by H. G. Johnson, and a further 'left-wing'
interpretation by Joan Robinson, as well as other essays which
help the reader to see Keynes as a man.

The monetarists seem to be as frugal with the printed word as
they would have the Government be with the money supply.
Easily accessible is the essay by Milton Friedman, 'Monetary
Theory and Policy', in *Inflation: Selected Readings*, edited by
R. J. Ballard and P. Doyle (Penguin, 1969). Another and com-
plementary summary by Milton Friedman is his lecture, 'The
Counter-Revolution in Monetary Theory' (Institute of Economic
Affairs, 1970). A really simple account of the way the government

actually manages the money supply and the national debt today has yet to be written. This is because everybody is still digesting the new procedures introduced in 1971 and foreshadowed in 'Competition and Credit control' (*Bank of England Quarterly Bulletin*, June 1971). There is a useful summary of the whole subject in *The UK Economy*, mentioned in the section on Chapters 7 and 9, and a key article by E. V. Morgan and R. L. Harrington, 'Reserve Assets and the Supply of Money' (*The Manchester School*, March 1973). Extracts from the writings of F. A. Hayek which give the essence of his forty-year running dispute with the ideas of Keynes are conveniently assembled in *A Tiger by the Tail*, compiled by S. R. Shenoy (Institute of Economic Affairs, 1972).

Appendix I
Statistical Sources and Methods

Table 1

Retail prices

This index, which has been used throughout to deflate money values to 1925 prices, is calculated from *The British Economy: Key Statistics 1900–1970* (London and Cambridge Economic Service, Department of Applied Economics, University of Cambridge). For the years 1970–74 I have used the *Department of Employment Gazette* (HMSO). The index and annual increases in prices are given in Appendix II.

National savings

The money series was simply calculated by applying the rates of interest compound as given in the text (page 50) to an initial investment of £100 for each successive year, 1925–73. The resulting totals were then deflated by the retail price index to give an index of the real value of savings.

Building society shares

This was calculated in the same way as national savings, but using the average interest rates given in Appendix II. For the period 1925–49 the source of these interest rates was 'The Perennial Problem of Interest Rates', by Herbert Ashworth (*Investors Chronicle*, 4 June 1959). From 1950–74 the source was *Financial Statistics* (HMSO and the Building Societies Association).

Industrial shares

The money series was based upon the price index and yields given in Appendix II. For 1925–70 the figures were taken from *The British Economy: Key Statistics* (see under 'Retail prices' in this section) and for 1971 onwards from *Financial Statistics* (see above). The price index from April 1962 and the yields from 1963 are in fact from the *Financial Times* 'Actuaries 500' industrial shares index.

The series excludes property and financial companies. In each successive year the dividend yield, less a uniform deduction of 38·75 per cent income tax, was added to the index value and then grossed up (or down) by the next change in the index. The assumption of a standard rate of tax means that taxation is over-allowed for in most of the period, especially pre-war. Capital gains taxation, however, has been ignored and no allowance was made for rights or scrip issues.

Older houses

I have used the index of older-house prices prepared by the Nationwide Building Society. The index, which is weighted by region, relates to Great Britain and is based on 1939 = 100. Over the period as a whole the prices of both old and new houses have moved similarly, and between 1939 and 1974 the difference is only 1·3 per cent. I have taken end-year prices except for 1974, which is end-September. There appears to be little information readily available on changes in house prices between the wars. Opinion, which I have taken, is that there was little change in money terms between 1925 and 1939; I have assumed this with some doubts but without any attempt at verification. The index used is reproduced in Appendix II.

Gold

The prices used are London bullion-market prices in pence per fine ounce. The figures for 1925–70 were supplied by Johnson Matthey Limited. From 1971 the source was the Bank of England *Quarterly Review*. Free-market prices were used from 1968, and the whole series is reproduced in Appendix II.

English furniture

The index number used was calculated from *Antiques as an Investment*, by R. H. Rush (Prentice-Hall, New York, 1968) for

1925–65, and from *Investments You Can Live with and Enjoy*, by the same author (Simon and Schuster, New York, 1974) for 1965–73. I have assumed on expert advice that prices did not change between 1973 and 1974. Mr Rush's indices, which represent averages of indices for Chippendale, Hepplewhite, Sheraton, Queen Anne, William and Mary, Jacobean and Adam pieces, are based on US prices and his detailed sources are not clear. It is perhaps a heroic assumption that US and UK prices of English furniture moved similarly over the period, but no other statistical source could be traced and the results are plausible.

Chart 1

The index of share prices and the retail price index used to deflate it are from the sources given above.

Chart 2

The data on which this chart is based were estimated by me from the sources given in the Notes on Further Reading.

Chart 5

The unemployment ratio for 1920–70 is taken from *The British Economy, Key Statistics*, (see under Table 1, 'Retail Prices in this appendix). It is total unemployment as a percentage of employees in employment. The series was completed from the *Monthly Digest of Statistics* (HMSO). The series is not uniform over the whole period. The GDP data are from the same source and brought up to date from *National Income and Expenditure 1963–73* (HMSO).

Appendix II

Selected Indicators of Output, Unemployment, Prices, Yields and Asset Values, 1925-74

	RETAIL PRICES		ORD. SHARE INDEX				2½% Consols					
YEAR 1963=100 (1)	% Increase over previous year (2)	1925=100 (3)	1925=100 at 1925 prices (4)	Dividend yield % (5)	Building Society shares average yield (6)	Gross flat yield £ (7)	Net price £ (8)	Older House prices 1939=100 (9)	London Gold price per fine oz. (10)	GDP at 1963 prices (11)	Unemployment (12)
1925	37	0·0	100	100		4·35	4·44	56·3		425·46	49	11·3
1926	36	(2·7)	104·8·	108	6·91	4·39	4·55	55·0		420·93	47	12·5
1927	35	(2·8)	109·5	115	6·12	4·39	4·56	54·9		420·93	51	9·7
1928	35	0·0	128·6	135	5·60	4·54	4·47	55·8		420·93	51	10·8
1929	35	0·0	123·8	130	6·13	4·54	4·60	54·3		420·95	52	10·4
1930	33	(5·7)	100·0	112	7·26	4·65	4·48	56·0		420·99	52	16·0
1931	31	(6·1)	81·0	96	8·03	4·62	4·39	55·2		460·52	49	21·3
1932	30	(3·2)	76·2	94	6·99	4·52	3·74	66·4		590·07	49	22·1
1933	30	0·0	90·5	112	5·27	3·95	3·39	73·8		620·87	52	19·9
1934	30	0·0	114·3	141	4·64	3·80	3·10	83·6		685·65	55	16·7
1935	30	0·0	123·8	153	4·65	3·64	2·89	87·2		710·10	57	15·5
1936	31	3·3	142·9	170	4·50	3·45	2·93	84·8		700·29	61	13·1
1937	32	3·2	133·3	155	5·10	3·38	3·28	79·0		700·73	62	10·8
1938	33	3·1	109·5	123	5·19	3·37	3·38	71·6		710·55	62	13·5
1939	34	3·0	104·8	114	6·50	3·40	3·72	66·1	100·0	770·34		11·6
1940	38	11·8	85·7	83	6·94	3·27	3·40	72·6		840·00		9·7
1941	42	10·5	90·5	72	6·19	2·83	3·13	79·8		840·00		6·6

Year												
1942	45		100.0	82	5.33	2.48	3.03	82.3		840.00		2.4
1943	47		119.0	94	4.58	2.40	3.10	80.8		840.00		0.8
1944	47		133.3	105	4.36	2.36	3.14	80.5		840.00		0.7
1945	49		138.1	105	4.19	2.34	2.92	86.9		860.25		1.2
1946	51		152.4	100	4.03	2.15	2.60	95.4		860.25	64.6	2.5
1947	54		157.1	108	4.57	2.15	2.76	89.6		860.25	65.1	3.1
1948	57		152.4	99	5.16	2.16	3.21	78.8		860.25	68.0	1.8
1949	59		142.9	90	5.66	2.15	3.30	73.5		860.25	70.4	1.6
1950	61	3.4	147.6	89	5.85	2.22	3.54	71.4		1,240.00	73.0	1.5
1951	67	9.8	171.4	95	6.61	2.22	3.78	65.8		1,240.00	74.6	1.2
1952	73	9.0	142.9	73	7.16	2.38	4.23	58.5		1,240.00	74.1	2.1
1953	75	2.7	152.4	75	6.92	2.45	4.08	61.8	284.3	1,240.00	77.1	1.8
1954	76	1.3	200.0	98	6.19	2.46	3.75	66.6	278.8	1,250.92	80.3	1.5
1955	80	5.3	233.3	108	6.17	2.61	4.17	60.8	291.2	1,250.28	83.0	1.2
1956	83.8	4.8	219.0	97	7.00	3.08	4.73	53.3	300.4	1,250.28	83.8	1.3
1957	86.9	3.7	233.3	99	6.91	3.45	4.49	49.6	306.4	1,250.21	85.3	1.6
1958	89.5	3.0	238.1	98	7.07	3.48	5.00	49.8	312.6	1,245.79	85.2	2.2
1959	90.1	0.7	342.9	141	5.27	3.43	4.95	51.1	328.1	1,245.86	89.0	2.3
1960	91.0	1.0	433.6	176	4.81	3.37	5.35	46.7	353.9	1,255.19	93.8	1.7
1961	94.1	3.4	449.6	177	5.34	3.54	6.25	40.3	398.8	1,250.98	95.5	1.6
1962	98.0	4.1	419.0	158	5.70	3.70	6.05	41.8	412.9	1,250.09	96.8	2.1
1963	100.0	2.0	476.2	176	4.93	3.51	5.70	44.2	450.9	1,250.58	100.0	2.6
1964	103.2	3.2	509.5	183	4.63	3.50	6.03	41.5	484.6	1,255.32	105.8	1.7
1965	108.1	4.7	476.2	163	5.54	3.78	6.42	39.0	519.7	1,255.28	108.6	1.5
1966	112.4	4.0	481.0	158	5.67	4.01	6.80	36.7	545.0	1,255.75	110.5	1.6
1967	115.2	2.5	514.3	165	5.10	4.20	6.69	37.4	594.1	1,280.43	112.2	2.5
1968	120.6	4.7	728.6	224	3.69	4.37	7.39	33.8	634.6	1,635.55	116.6	2.5
1969	127.2	5.5	719.0	207	3.90	4.82	8.88	28.2	674.6	1,751.86	119.3	2.5
1970	135.3	6.4	633.3	173	4.52	4.94	9.16	27.3	728.0	1,500.18	121.3	2.6
1971	148.0	9.4	880.3	220	3.96	4.95	9.05	27.6	864.4	1,642.00	122.9	3.5
1972	158.6	7.2	1,019.0	238	3.31	4.88	9.11	27.5	1,214.7	1,997.86	126.1	3.9
1973	173.1	9.1	882.2	183	4.10	6.51	10.85	23.2	1,397.8	4,065.74	132.6	2.7
1974	201.1	16.1	487.6	90	8.00	7.50	14.95		1,477.0	6,837.00	131.4	2.7

SOURCE: see Appendix I.

Appendix III

Average London Gold Prices at Daily Fixings, Monthly, 1969–74

Year	Jan.	Feb.	March	April	May	June	July	Aug.	Sept.	Oct.	Nov.	Dec.	Year
1969	42·3	42·6	43·2	43·3	43·5	41·4	41·8	41·1	40·9	40·6	37·4	35·2	41·1
1970	34·9	35·0	35·1	35·6	36·0	35·4	35·2	35·4	36·2	37·5	37·4	37·4	36·0
1971	37·9	38·7	38·9	39·0	40·5	40·1	40·9	42·7	42·0	42·5	42·9	43·5	40·8
1972	45·7	48·3	48·3	49·0	54·6	62·1	65·6	67·0	65·6	64·8	62·8	63·8	58·2
1973	65·1	74·1	84·2	90·5	101·8	120·0	102·3	106·5	103·0	100·0	94·8	106·5	97·2
1974	129·1	150·1	168·4	172·2	163·4	154·1	142·6	154·5	151·7	158·7	181·6	183·8	159·2

SOURCE: 1969–73, Samuel Montagu & Co., *Annual Bullion Review, 1974*, Sharps Pixley Ltd, *Monthly Market Report*

Index

Money supply (money stock), 139, 143–6
Multinational companies, 129
Multiplier, 96–8, 133–4

National income, 107n., 127
Neo-Keynesians, *see* Keynesians
Net output, definition of, 118

Oil prices, 21, 130, 131
Organization for Economic Cooperation and Development (OECD), 22, 92
Overseas investment, *see* Investment
Ownership and control, separation of, 16–17, 121

Paper assets, *see* Assets
Pensions, 30–32
Pensioners, *see* Retired people
Pigou, A. C., *see* Pigou effect
Pigou effect, 135
Planned sector, 16–17
Post-competitive sector, *see* Planned sector
Post Office Savings Bank (POSB), 47–50
Power economics, *see* Economics of power
Prais, S. J., 118
Premium bonds, 57n.
Price mechanism, 98, 146, 150, 152
Professional advice, importance of, 46, 65, 79
Profits, 121, 127, 150
Property, 26; abroad, 82; as an investment, 64–5, 79, 80–82

Quality of products, 34–5

Rates, local authority, 41–2
Real returns, 44; antiques, 83–4; assurance, 57–60; deposits, 47–50; DIY, 39–41; equities, 52–3; fixed-interest securities, 50–52; freezers, 38–9; gold, 74; hoarding, 38; property, 80–82; Retirement Certificates, 63–4; SAYE, 64; summarized, 84–6; unit trusts, 53–6
Redeemable securities, 44
Rent, 127
Retailing, 28, 36–8
Retired people, 30–32
Retirement Certificates, 63–4
Returns, real, *see* Real returns
Reverse yield gap, *see* Yield
Risk, 45–6
Roeber, Joe, 109

Save As You Earn (SAYE), 64
Savings, 133–4, 137, 142; personal, 43
Schultz, Harry D., 66
Self-employed persons, 27–9, 126–7
Self-sufficiency, 39–41, 85
Shareholders, 119
Shares, *see* Equities
Silver, 76–7
Slump, 15–16
Slump-flation, 16
Small businesses, 27–9, 36–8, 117–20, 125, 127
Smaller Businesses Association, 29
Social costs, 150
Social security contributions, 27
Social strife, 24, 85
Special Drawing Rights (SDRs), 129

More about Penguins and Pelicans

Penguinews, which appears every month, contains details of all the new books issued by Penguins as they are published. From time to time it is supplemented by *Penguins in Print*, which is a complete list of all titles available. (There are some five thousand of these.)

A specimen copy of *Penguinews* will be sent to you free on request. For a year's issues (including the complete lists) please send 50p if you live in the British Isles, or 75p if you live elsewhere. Just write to Dept EP, Penguin Books Ltd, Harmondsworth, Middlesex, enclosing a cheque or postal order, and your name will be added to the mailing list.

In the U.S.A.: For a complete list of books available from Penguin in the United States write to Dept CS, Penguin Books Inc., 7110 Ambassador Road, Baltimore, Maryland 21207.

In Canada: For a complete list of books available from Penguin in Canada write to Penguin Books Canada Ltd, 41 Steelcase Road West, Markham, Ontario.

Economics and the Public Purpose

John Kenneth Galbraith

The concept of private affluence amid public squalor first introduced in *The Affluent Society* has 'conditioned the thinking of half a generation', to quote Michael Stewart in *The Times*. Later *The New Industrial State* drew attention to a technostructure of managerial experts more powerful than the people.

Now in *Economics and the Public Purpose* J. K. Galbraith marshals and summarizes his arguments to underline the flaws in neo-classical economics. Tracing the real and unreal workings of the market, from the grass-roots of shop and housewife to the vast and often anti-social operations of the modern corporation, he finally prescribes a 'New Socialism' of state control by way of reform.

Moreover Galbraith's quick sense of ridicule, his wit and his gift for exposition are as lively as ever in a sparkling book that, according to *Tribune,* 'should be read by all whose socialist convictions may fall away when they reach high office'.

Not for sale in the U.S.A. or Canada

The Affluent Society

John Kenneth Galbraith

Second Edition

Wittily, gracefully, devastatingly, Professor Galbraith attacks our most cherished economic myths. Why worship work and productivity if many of the goods we produce are superfluous – artificial 'needs' created by high-pressure advertising? Why grudge expenditure on vital public works while ignoring waste and extravagance in the private sector of the economy? Classical economics was born in a harsh world of mass poverty, and it has left us with a set of preconceptions hard to adapt to the realities of our own richer age. And so, too often, 'the bland lead the bland'. Our unfamiliar problems need a new approach, and the reception given to this already famous book has shown the value of its fresh, lively ideas.

'The most entertaining and profound exposure of post-war Western society that has yet been published' – Richard Crossman, M.P.

'He shows himself a truly sensitive and civilized man, whose ideas are grounded in the common culture of the two continents, and may serve as a link between them; his book is of foremost importance for them both' – *The Times Literary Supplement*

Not for sale in the U.S.A. or Canada

Modern Economics

J. Pen

In 1936 Keynes published his famous *General Theory of Employment, Interest and Money*, and the science of economics has never been the same since. Gone is the comfortable 'classical' belief in a self-adjusting balance between supply and demand; moreover, allied to Keynesian theory, the growth of exact quantitative economics has tended to produce a distinct 'modern economics'. A silent revolution has occurred.

It is widely held that Keynesian theories can only be comprehended by the expert, and this in itself delays the application of modern ideas, since every citizen, when he shops, works, or votes, is a practising economist. Professor Pen, the well-known Dutch economist, challenges this assumption in this Pelican, in which he sets out to explain to the non-expert the meaning of Keynes's ideas and the findings of modern statistical methods.

His book provides a clear (and frequently humorous and hard-hitting) introduction to modern theories regarding international trade, national budgets, the function of money inflation and deflation, wages, economic growth, and many other economic topics in daily discussion.

Guide to the British Economy

Peter Donaldson

Third Edition – Revised

Guide to the British Economy is intended for the general
reader who would like to have some grasp of what
economics is about and what makes the economy tick, but
who may find the textbook approach unpalatably abstract.
Economic ideas, therefore, are presented here within the
real context of the British economy. The aim is both to
give an impression of the working of the different elements
in the economy, and to illustrate the extent to which
economic analysis can be helpful in solving the problems
which face policy-makers.

In the first part of this introductory guide Peter
Donaldson is mainly concerned with matters of finance,
including the stock-market. After a full examination of
industry, labour, and trade, he goes on, in the final
section of the book, to a general discussion of economic
theories, their scope, and limitations.

This highly readable text raises and discusses sensibly
and constructively the large and controversial economic
arguments that rumble on day after day in our
newspapers and in front of the television cameras' – *The
Times Educational Supplement*.

'An excellent little book. It provides a most lucid and
absorbing survey of the British Economy for the
intelligent layman or for the beginning student of
economics. It really cannot be faulted in either its scope
or its exposition' – Professor Lomax in the *Economic
Journal*